The Vimalakīrti Nirdeśa Sūtra

Distributed in the Commonwealth and Europe
by Routledge & Kegan Paul Ltd
London and Henley-on-Thames

THE VIMALAKĪRTI NIRDEŚA SŪTRA

(Wei Mo Chieh So Shuo Ching)

TRANSLATED BY

Lu K'uan Yü (Charles Luk)

THE CLEAR LIGHT SERIES

SHAMBALA
BERKELEY AND LONDON

FIRST PUBLISHED IN 1972
BY SHAMBALA PUBLICATIONS INC
1409 FIFTH STREET
BERKELEY, CALIFORNIA 94710
& BARN COTTAGE, STERT
DEVIZES, WILTSHIRE

MADE AND PRINTED IN GREAT BRITAIN
BY T. & A. CONSTABLE LTD
EDINBURGH

ISBN 0 87773-035-0
LIBRARY OF CONGRESS CATALOGUE 71-189851

This book is published in THE CLEAR LIGHT SERIES
Dedicated to W. Y. Evans-Wentz.
The series is under the general editorship of
Samuel Bercholz and Michael Fagan.

Respectfully dedicated to
THE VENERABLE UPĀSAKA W. B. PICARD,
Head of the Mousehole Buddhist Group,
Mousehole, Cornwall, England,
whose encouragement has sustained my
humble efforts to present translations of
Chinese Buddhist texts
to keen students of the Dharma
in the West

Contents

Foreword

We take refuge in the Buddha,
We take refuge in the Dharma,
We take refuge in the Saṅgha,
We take refuge in the Triple Gem within ourselves.

THE Sanskrit title "The Vimalakīrti Nirdeśa Sūtra" means *The Sūtra spoken by Vimalakīrti* which is also called *A Dharma door to Inconceivable Liberation.* The first title shows the speaker who initiated this sūtra and the second reveals the method of practice leading to inconceivable liberation, the aim of all Bodhisattvas.

Our translation is based on explanations and annotations by the enlightened Indian translator Kumārajīva and his equally enlightened Chinese pupil and assistant, Seng Chao, author of the well-known treatise Chao Lun, and on the commentary in 1630 by Ch'an master Po Shan of the Ming dynasty.

According to Kumārajīva, Vimalakīrti came from the realm of Profound Joy of Akṣobhya Buddha to perform his work of salvation on this earth. He initiated this sūtra by sending his followers, a group of five hundred sons of the elders at Vaiśālī, to the Buddha to receive His instructions, while he himself lay sick at home, awaiting his turn to enlighten the Bodhisattvas, the chief disciples of the Buddha, the devas and men.

This sūtra is divided into fourteen chapters.

Chapter 1 praises the Bodhisattvas present whose meritorious deeds had transformed their worlds into pure lands and who were qualified to convert and liberate living beings. Those coming to the assembly included devas, the eight classes of spiritual beings[1] and monks, nuns, male and female devotees.

Sent by Vimalakīrti to the assembly were an elder called Ratna-rāśi with five hundred sons of the elders at Vaiśālī, each with a canopy to offer to the Buddha as a mark of respect to Him. The World Honoured One used His transcendental power to transform all these canopies into a large one covering all the worlds with their Buddhas expounding the Dharma in the ten directions. This shows the inconceivable state of the Buddha land to induce Hīnayāna men to develop the boundless Mahāyāna mind to win the pure land.

Thereat, Ratna-rāśi praised the Buddha in a long gāthā, adding that the five hundred sons of the elders had set their minds on the quest of supreme enlightenment and praying the Buddha to teach them how to win His pure land, the first step towards realizing the absolute state of enlightenment.

The Buddha then taught that the pure land resulted from how they converted and brought to perfection all living beings, for this immaculate land came from the straightforward mind, the profound mind, the Mahāyāna mind, the practice of the six perfections (pāramitās), of the four infinite minds, of the fourfold Bodhisattva action to befriend and liberate living beings, and of expedient methods (upāya), the application of the thirty-seven contributory stages to enlightenment, the dedicating of all merits won to self-enlightenment and the enlightenment of others, the preaching of how to eradicate the eight obstructing evil

[1] The eight classes of spiritual beings: see the author's Ch'an and Zen Teaching, Third Series, *The Sūtra of Complete Enlightenment*, p. 278, n. 3. (Rider, London; Shambala, Berkeley.)

states so that the Dharma is accessible to everyone, the keeping of commandments and non-committal of the ten evils.

As the Buddha's teaching aroused in Śāriputra's mind strong doubt about the unclean state of this Buddha land, that is the world, the Buddha knew of his thought and pressed the toes of His feet on the ground and suddenly this world became pure and clean in all its majesty. He then said to the disciple: "This Buddha land of mine is always pure and clean but appears filthy so that I can lead people of inferior spirituality to their salvation."

On this occasion, Ratna-rāśi and his five hundred followers realized the patient endurance of the uncreate while many others present either won the Dharma eye or put an end to the stream of transmigration.

Thus the World Honoured One revealed the pure and clean Buddha land in all its majesty, the realization of which is the aim of all Bodhisattvas, as outlined in this introductory chapter.

Chapter 2 lists the meritorious deeds achieved by Vimalakīrti, the initiator of this important Mahāyāna sūtra, who appeared as an elderly upāsaka at Vaiśālī to give a good example of the practice of the six perfections or pāramitās through charity, discipline, forbearance, devotion, meditation and wisdom, and of Bodhisattva lines of conduct. Now using upāya or the expedient method he appeared indisposed to receive and urge thousands of visitors who came to enquire after his health, to seek supreme enlightenment.

Chapter 3 tells of the chief disciples who were ordered by the Buddha to call on Vimalakīrti to enquire after his health on His behalf and who all spoke of their previous encounters with the upāsaka which showed that they were not qualified to meet him again.

This very interesting chapter should be read by all students who have practised Hīnayāna in their quest of relative nirvāṇa, to advance further on the Mahāyāna path in order to reach the absolute nirvāṇa. For the purpose of Vimalakīrti's teaching in this chapter is to urge the Buddha's disciples of the śrāvaka stage to develop the Mahāyāna mind in order to realize supreme enlightenment.

Chapter 4 tells why the Bodhisattvas who had not reached the highest degree of enlightenment, also declined to call on Vimalakīrti to enquire after his health on behalf of the Buddha because they were not qualified for the visit after their experiences of previous confrontations with the upāsaka.

This chapter is also indispensable for those training in Bodhisattva development into Buddhahood for it teaches what they should know and do in their practice.

Chapter 5 describes Mañjuśrī's vivid encounter with Vimalakīrti as his equal in debate.

This is the most fascinating chapter in which Vimalakīrti remained speechless when asked by Mañjuśrī about the non-dual Dharma, that is the absolute state of thatness which is beyond words and speech. It has been widely commented on and discussed in all great monasteries throughout China since Kumārajīva translated this sūtra into Chinese.

Chapter 6 explains the realization of inconceivable liberation through the performance of the highest merits that comprise the lion throne of a Buddha, which is the foundation of enlightenment. To show the profound functioning of inconceivable liberation, Vimalakīrti used his transcendental power to beg the Buddha Merukalpa to send to his house thirty-two thousand high, large, majestic and spotless lion thrones which were all contained in his room without hindering anything at Vaiśālī, in the world and in the four heavens where all things remained unchanged as before.

Mañjuśrī and the Bodhisattvas who had achieved inconceivable liberation could easily sit on the high thrones, whereas those of the śrāvaka stage could not and had to pay reverence to the Tathāgata Merukalpa and develop the Mahāyāna mind before they could do so.

Vimalakīrti taught this inconceivable liberation which wipes out space and time, to agree with the indescribable and inexpressible state of absolute thatness.

The aim of this chapter is to reveal the wonders of inconceivable liberation to those of the śrāvaka stage and to urge them to seek supreme enlightenment.

Chapter 7 tells how to practise Mahāyāna in order to win inconceivable liberation. It contains the fascinating dialogue between two great Bodhisattvas, Vimalakīrti and Mañjuśrī, and teaches the correct way of looking at living beings who are fundamentally illusory and non-existent, and how to adjust their non-existence with the Bodhisattva lines of conduct such as the application of the four infinite states of mind (i.e. kindness, compassion, joy and indifference) without expectation of reward; the defeat of birth and death; the winning of support from the Tathāgata's moral merits by liberating all living beings from troubles and their causes, by upholding right mindfulness, by advocating the unborn and the undying, by means of non-rising evil and unending good, the root of which is the body which comes into being because of craving caused by discrimination born from inverted thinking, which arises from nothingness.

To enhance the correctness of the teaching, a goddess appeared to shower flowers which, when falling on the Bodhisattvas, dropped immediately to the ground, but stuck to the bodies of the disciples (of the śrāvaka stage) who could not shake them off because of their differentiation between the flowers (i.e. form) and the absolute (formlessness) which they sought. She taught the disciples to stop all differentiation so that they could wipe out space and time to agree with supreme enlightenment.

Chapter 8 tells how to enter the Buddha path which leads to supreme enlightenment and which is accessible only to a pure and clean mind.

A few years ago a book reviewer wrongly criticized me for translating the technical term ch'ing chin hsin by *pure and clean mind* instead of "unmixed mind" which, he argued, implies a mind "devoid of objects" without realizing that the "pure and clean-mind" is not only "pure" but remains "clean", that is, immune from defilements in the course of his training and also when appearing in all realms of existence to perform his work of salvation. For example, a crystal ball, though unmixed, is covered with mud when dropped on wet ground, and so becomes "pure but unclean".

So, this chapter explains that a Bodhisattva, in order to enter the Buddha path, should do his salvation-work without being contaminated with ignorance, arrogance and pride in the world of animals, with irritation and anger when appearing in the hells, etc. In other words, he should be free from all discrimination as expounded in the text in order to realize the pure and clean mind.

This chapter, which contains a very interesting and fascinating dialogue between Vimalakīrti and Mañjuśrī, and the former's exposition of this freedom from discrimination in a long gāthā, is too long and elaborate to be condensed in a short foreword. Readers are, therefore, urged to study it carefully in order to free themselves from defilements caused by discrimination in order to tread the enlightened path of all Buddhas. But the ending of discrimination is possible only by initiation to the non-dual Dharma which is fully explained in the next chapter.

In *Chapter 9*, Vimalakīrti invited all the Bodhisattvas present to speak of their understanding of the non-dual Dharma, that is, about their realization of the absolute state beyond all dualities, relativities and contraries, the main causes that create all living beings and their worlds. After Mañjuśrī had summed up by declaring that that state is reached when it is no longer within the province of word, speech, indication and intellect, he asked Vimalakīrti to give his enlightened opinion on it. The latter kept silent without saying a word to show real initiation to the indescribable and inexpressible thatness.

The non-dual Dharma realized by Vimalakīrti would be incomplete if it could not perform its function which is commonly called supernatural power. Hence in *Chapter 10* Vimalakīrti used it to show to the assembly the Fragrant Land with its Buddha and Bodhisattvas and to create an illusory messenger to go there to beg for fragrant rice from that Buddha for the purpose of using it to convert to Mahāyāna the śrāvakas at Vaiśālī. Vimalakīrti also took this opportunity to teach the visiting Bodhisattvas from the Fragrant Land by praising and revealing to them the Dharma preached by Śākyamuni Buddha in this world.

Chapter 11 tells of Vimalakīrti and Mañjuśrī, together with the disciples and Bodhisattvas going to Āmravana park to call on the Buddha who was expounding the Dharma there.

The Buddha welcomed them and taught Ānanda that all Buddhas and Bodhisattvas do their work of salvation in many ways, and by means of all things to open up the Dharma doors to enlightenment. He also urged him to refrain from all discrimination under all circumstances.

The Buddha also taught the visiting Bodhisattvas from the Fragrant Land the exhaustible and inexhaustible Dharmas which they should always bear in mind.

In *Chapter 12* the Buddha urged Vimalakīrti to say how he would see Him impartially.[1] Vimalakīrti's long reply is interesting in that it dealt with the correct way of perceiving the Buddha.

The Buddha then revealed that Vimalakīrti had come from the realm of Profound Joy of Akṣobhya Buddha and ordered him to show it to the assembly, which he did as described in the text.[2]

Thus the Buddha land is accessible to anybody whose mind is pure and clean and is set on the quest of supreme enlightenment and the practice of Mahāyāna as taught in this important sūtra.

Chapter 13 tells of Śakra, lord of the thirty-three heavens, who praised the inconceivable liberation taught in this sūtra and vowed to protect all believers and practisers of its Dharma. The Buddha praised Śakra's high opinion of the sūtra from which the enlightenment of all Buddhas originated.

The Buddha then related His own case when in a former life, he was an elder's son called Lunar Canopy and was urged by the Tathāgata Bhaiṣajya to make an offering of (or teach to others) this inconceivable Dharma which surpasses all other forms of offering. This means that of all kinds of bestowals that of the doctrine of supreme enlightenment is

[1] As Vimalakīrti had told Mañjuśrī to come and see the Tathāgata the Buddha now urged him to teach those present how to perceive Him. Chapter 7 has taught the correct way of looking at living beings and this Chapter 12 now teaches how to look at the Tathāgata.

[2] Vimalakīrti performed the profound function of showing his own realm of Profound Joy to the assembly to stimulate their efforts to seek supreme enlightenment.

the best. As a result of this practice, He realized the patient endurance of the uncreate and received the Tathāgata Bhaiṣajya's prophecy that He would later achieve enlightenment.

His father, Precious Canopy, later became a Buddha called Precious Flame, and the latter's one thousand sons were the thousand Buddhas of Bhadrakalpa or the Virtuous Aeon, among whom Lunar Canopy became Śākyamuni Buddha.[1]

Chapter 14 tells of the Buddha's injunction to Maitreya, the next Buddha on earth, to spread this sūtra widely.

The Buddha spoke of those who prefer proud words and racy styles, thus foretelling the majority of modern scholars everywhere who do not take the trouble to dig out the profound meanings of sūtras but are only interested in holding endless and sterile discussions which intensify discrimination and keep them far from supreme enlightenment.

Readers who have studied the Diamond Sūtra, the Heart Sūtra, the Sūtra of Complete Enlightenment and the Śūraṅgama Sūtra which we have presented, are urged to read this sūtra which is complementary to them and will help the student to understand better the Mahāyāna Dharma.

Now that some Western Buddhists have made very good progress in their meditation thereby achieving serenity (dhyāna) and even realizing spiritual awakening (satori) they should guard against falling into the stages of the śrāvaka and Pratyeka-buddha by starting their immediate training in Bodhisattva development into Buddhahood as taught in this important sūtra. For it is a matter for regret to be contented with little progress which cannot lead to supreme

[1] See Ch'an and Zen Teaching, second series, part I, the Forty Transmission gāthās, pp. 29-31. (Rider, London; Shambala, Berkeley.)

enlightenment, and to shun the sacred duty of planting the Mahāyāna banner in the Occident in the present Dharma ending age.

Upāsaka Lu K'uan Yü

Hongkong,
The Year of the Dog (1970)

CHAPTER ONE

The Buddha Land

THUS have I heard. Once upon a time the Buddha sojourned in the Āmra park at Vaiśālī with an assembly of eight thousand great bhikṣus. With them were thirty-two thousand Bodhisattvas who were well known for having achieved all the perfections[1] that lead to the great wisdom.[2] They had received instructions from many Buddhas and formed a Dharma-protecting citadel. By upholding the right Dharma, they could give the lion's roar (to teach others); so their names were heard in the ten directions. They were not invited but came to the assembly to spread the teaching on the Three Treasures to transmit it in perpetuity. They had overcome all demons and defeated heresies, and their deeds, words and thoughts were pure and clean, being free from the (five) hindrances[3] and the (ten) bonds.[4] They had realized serenity of mind[5] and had achieved unimpeded liberation. They had achieved right concentration and mental stability, thereby acquiring the uninterrupted power of speech. They had achieved all the (six) pāramitās: charity

[1] i.e. the six pāramitās (charity, discipline, patience, devotion, serenity and wisdom) and six transcendental powers (divine sight, divine hearing, knowledge of the minds of all living beings, knowledge of all forms of previous existences of self and others, power to appear at will in any place and to have absolute freedom and insight into the ending of the stream of transmigration).

[2] i.e. Buddha-wisdom.

[3] The five hindrances or covers are: desire, anger, drowsiness, excitability and doubt.

[4] The ten bonds are: shamelessness, unblushingness, envy, meanness, regretfulness, torpidity, unstableness, gloominess, anger and secret sinning.

[5] i.e. the seventh stage of non-retrogression in the Bodhisattva development into Buddhahood.

(dāna), discipline (śīla), patience (kṣānti), devotion (vīrya), serenity (dhyāna) and wisdom (prajñā), as well as the expedient method (upāya) of teaching. However, to them these realizations did not mean any gain whatsoever for themselves, so that they were in line with the patient endurance of the uncreate (anutpattika-dharma-kṣānti). They were able to turn the wheel of the Law that never turns back. Being able to interpret the (underlying nature of) phenomena, they knew very well the roots (propensities) of all living beings; they surpassed them all and realized fearlessness. They had cultivated their minds by means of merits and wisdom with which they embellished their physical features which were unsurpassable, thus giving up all earthly adornments. Their towering reputation exceeded the height of Mount Sumeru. Their profound faith (in the uncreate) was unbreakable like a diamond. Their treasures of the Dharma illuminated all lands and rained down nectar. Their speeches were profound and unsurpassable. They entered deep into all (worldly) causes but cut off all heretical views for they were already free from all dualities and had rooted out all (previous) habits. They were fearless and gave the lion's roar to proclaim the Dharma, their voices being like thunder. They could not be gauged for they were beyond all measures. They had amassed all treasures of the Dharma and acted like (skilful) seafaring pilots. They were well versed in the profound meanings of all Dharmas. They knew very well the mental states of all living beings and their comings and goings (within the realms of existence). They had reached the state near the unsurpassed sovereign wisdom of all Buddhas, having acquired the ten fearless powers (daśabala) giving complete knowledge[1] and the

[1] Daśabala or the ten fearless powers that give complete knowledge of: 1, what is right or wrong in every condition; 2, what is the karma of every

eighteen different characteristics (of a Buddha as compared with Bodhisattvas (āveṇikadharma).[1] Although they were free from (rebirth in) evil existences, they appeared in five mortal realms as royal physicians to cure all ailments, prescribing the right medicine in each individual case, thereby winning countless merits to embellish countless Buddha lands. Each living being derived great benefit from seeing and hearing them, for their deeds were not in vain. Thus they had achieved all excellent merits.

Their names were: the Bodhisattva Beholding All Things As Equal, the Bodhisattva Beholding All Things As Unequal, the Bodhisattva Beholding All Things As Equal Yet As Unequal, the Bodhisattva of Sovereign Serenity, the Bodhisattva of Sovereign Dharma, the Bodhisattva of Dharma-aspects, the Bodhisattva of Light, the Bodhisattva of Glorious Light, the Bodhisattva of Great Majesty, the Bodhisattva Store of Treasures, the Bodhisattva Store of Rhetoric, the Bodhisattva of Precious Hands, the Bodhisattva of Precious Mudrā, the Hand Raising Bodhisattva, the Hand Lowering Bodhisattva, the Always Grieved Bodhisattva, the Bodhisattva Root of Joy, the Bodhisattva Prince of Joy, the Bodhisattva Discerner of Sound, the Bodhisattva Womb of Space, the Bodhisattva Holding the Precious Torch, the Bodhisattva of Precious Boldness, the

---

being, past, future and present; 3, all stages of liberation through dhyāna and samādhi; 4, the good and evil roots of all beings; 5, the knowledge and understanding of every being; 6, the actual condition of every individual; 7, the direction and consequences of all laws; 8, all causes of mortality and of good and evil in their reality; 9, the former lives of all beings and the stage of nirvāṇa; and 10, the destruction of all illusion of every kind.

[1] Āveṇikadharma or the eighteen unsurpassed characteristics of a Buddha: his perfection of body (deeds), mouth (speech) and mind (thought), impartiality to all, serenity, self-sacrifice, unceasing desire to save, unflaggingly zeal therein, unfailing thought thereto, wisdom in it, powers of deliverance, the principle of it, revealing perfect wisdom in deed, word and thought, perfect knowledge of past, future and present.

Bodhisattva of Precious Insight, the Bodhisattva of Indrajāla,[1] the Bodhisattva Net of Light, the Bodhisattva of Causeless Contemplation, the Bodhisattva of Accumulated Wisdom, the Bodhisattva Precious Conqueror, the Bodhisattva King of Heavens, the Bodhisattva Destroyer of Demons, the Bodhisattva with Lightning Merits, the Bodhisattva of Sovereign Comfort, the Bodhisattva of Majestic Merits, the Bodhisattva of the Lion's Roar, the Bodhisattva of Thundering Voice, the Bodhisattva with a Voice like Rocks Knocking One Another, the Bodhisattva Fragrant Elephant, the Bodhisattva White Fragrant Elephant, the Bodhisattva of Constant Devotion, the Bodhisattva of Unremitting Care, the Bodhisattva of Wonderful Rebirth, the Bodhisattva Garland, the Bodhisattva Avalokiteśvara, the Bodhisattva Mahāsthāma, the Bodhisattva Brahma-jāla, the Bodhisattva of Precious Staff, the Unconquerable Bodhisattva, the Bodhisattva of Majestic Land, the Bodhisattva with a Golden Topknot, the Bodhisattva with a Pearl in His Topknot, the Bodhisattva Maitreya, the Bodhisattva Mañjuśrī, and other Bodhisattvas numbering in all thirty-two thousand.

There were also ten thousand Brahma-devas including Mahādeva Śikhin, coming from the four quarters to hear about the Dharma.

There were as well twelve thousand kings of heavens who came from the four quarters to sit in the assembly.

There were also other devas of awe-inspiring majesty, dragons, spirits, yakṣas, gandhāras, asuras, garuḍas, kinnaras and mahoragas who came to sit in the assembly.[2]

[1] The net of Indra, hanging in his hall, out of which all things can be produced.

[2] The eight classes of beings who always came to listen to the Buddha's preaching were: 1, the heavenly dragons; 2, heavenly spirits; 3, yakṣas or demons in the earth, air and lower heavens; 4, gandharvas, spirits on the

Many bhikṣus, bhikṣuṇīs, upāsakas and upāsikās also came to the assembly.[1]

Thus surrounded by an incalculable number of people circumambulating to pay their respects, the Buddha was about to expound the Dharma. Like the towering Mount Sumeru emerging from the great ocean, He sat comfortably on the lion throne eclipsing the imposing assembly.

A son of an elder (gṛhapati),[2] called Ratna-rāśi, came with five hundred sons of elders, with canopies decorated with the seven gems to pay respects and offer them to Him. By using His transcendental powers the Buddha transformed all the canopies into a single one which contained the great chiliocosm with Mount Sumeru and all the concentric ranges around it, great seas, rivers, streams, the sun, the moon, planets and stars, and the palaces of devas, dragons, and holy spirits appeared in the precious canopy which also covered all the Buddhas who were expounding the Dharma in the ten directions.

All those present who witnessed the Buddha's supernatural powers, praised the rare occurrence which they had never seen before, brought their palms together and gazed at Him without pausing for an instant.

Thereupon, Ratna-rāśi chanted the following gāthā of praise:

"I salute Him whose eyes are broad like the green
Lotus, whose mind is unchanging and serene,

---

fragrant mountains, so called because they do not drink wine or eat meat, but feed on incense and give off fragrant odours; 5, asuras or titans; 6, garuḍas, or mystical bird, the queen of the feathered race, enemy of the serpent race, and vehicle of Viṣṇu; 7, kinnaras, the musicians of kuveras (the gods of riches) with men's bodies and horses' heads; and 8, mahoragas, demons shaped like the boa.

[1] Monks, nuns, male and female devotees.

[2] Gṛhapati: an elder who is just, straightforward and honest.

Who has accumulated countless pure deeds that lead
All beings to the extinction of mortality.
I have seen the great saint use His transcendental powers
To create in the ten directions countless lands
In which Buddhas still proclaim the Dharma;
All this has the assembly seen and heard.
The power of thy Dharma surpasses all
Beings and bestows on them the wealth of the Law.
With great skill thou discernest all
Whilst unmoved in Reality.
Thou art from all phenomena released;
Hence to the King of Dharma I bow down.
Thou teacheth neither *is* nor *is not*
For all things by causes are created.
There is neither self nor doing nor thing done,
But good or evil karma is infallible.
Under the bo tree thou conquered Māra, obtained
Ambrosia, realized Nirvāṇa and won Bodhi.
From mind, thought and feeling art thou free
Thereby overcoming heresies,
Turning thrice in the chiliocosm the wheel
Of the Law that is pure and clean at heart.
To this gods and men who were saved attested.
Thus the Three Treasures appeared in the sahā world
To save living beings with this profound Dharma
Which, when applied, fails never to Nirvāṇa lead.
Thou art the king physician who destroys old age, illness and death.
So thine unfathomable Dharma of boundless merits I salute
While like Mount Sumeru thou art unmoved by both praise and censure.
Thy compassion is extended to both good and evil men,

Like space thy mind remains impartial. Does not anyone
Revere this human Buddha after hearing about Him?
I have offered Him a small canopy
Which encloses the great chiliocosm
With palaces of gods, dragons and spirits,
Gandhāras, yakṣas and others such as well
As all kings in this world. With mercy
He used His 'ten powers'[1] to make this change.
The witnesses praise the Buddha. I bow
To the most Honoured One in the three realms.
The whole assembly (now) take refuge in the King of
The Law. Those gazing at Him are filled with joy,
Each seeing the Bhagavat before him; 'tis
One of His eighteen characteristics.[2]
When He proclaims the Dharma with unchanging voice
All beings understand according to their natures
Saying the Bhagavat speaks their own languages;
'Tis one of His eighteen characteristics.
When He expounds the Dharma in one voice
They understand according to their versions
Deriving great benefit from what they have gathered;
This is one more of His eighteen characteristics.
When He expounds the Dharma in one voice
Some are filled with fear, others are joyful,
Some hate it while others are from doubts relieved;
'Tis one of His eighteen characteristics.
I bow to the Possessor of 'ten powers',[3]
I bow to Him who has achieved fearlessness
Acquiring all eighteen characteristics.
I bow to Him who guides others like a pilot;

[1] The Buddha's ten fearless powers: see p. 2, n. 1.
[2] The eighteen unsurpassed characteristics of a Buddha: see p. 3, n. 1.
[3] The ten powers (daśabala): see p. 2, n. 1.

I bow to Him who has untied all bonds;
I bow to Him who has reached the other shore;
I bow to Him who can all worlds deliver;
I bow to Him who from birth and death is free,
Who knows how living beings come and go,
And penetrates all things to win His freedom,
Who, skilful in nirvāṇic deeds
Cannot be soiled like the lotus,
Who plumbs the depths of everything without hindrance.
I bow to Him who, like space, relies on nothing."

After chanting the gāthā, Ratna-rāśi said to the Buddha: "World Honoured One, these five hundred sons of elders have set their minds on seeking supreme enlightenment (anuttara-samyak-saṁbodhi); they all wish to know how to win the pure and clean land of the Buddha. Will the World Honoured One teach us the Bodhisattva deeds that lead to the realization of the Pure Land?"

The Buddha said: "Excellent, Ratna-rāśi, it is good that you can ask on behalf of these Bodhisattvas about deeds that lead to the realization of the Buddha's Pure Land. Listen carefully and ponder over all what I now tell you."

Thereat, Ratna-rāśi and the five hundred sons of elders listened attentively to His instruction.

The Buddha said: "Ratna-rāśi, all species of living beings are the Buddha land sought by all Bodhisattvas. Why is it so? Because a Bodhisattva wins the Buddha land according to the living beings converted by him (to the Dharma); according to the living beings tamed by him; according to the country (where they will be reborn to) realize the Buddha-wisdom and in which they will grow the Bodhisattva root. Why is it so? Because a Bodhisattva wins the pure land solely for the benefit of all living beings. For instance, a man can build palaces and houses on vacant ground without difficulty, but he will fail if he attempts to build them in (empty) space. So, a Bodhisattva, in order to bring living beings to perfection, seeks the Buddha land which cannot be sought in (empty) space.

"Ratna-rāśi, you should know that the straightforward mind is the Bodhisattva's pure land, for when he realizes Buddhahood, beings who do not flatter will be reborn in his land.

"The profound mind is the Bodhisattva's pure land, for when he realizes Buddhahood living beings who have accumulated all merits will be reborn there.

"The Mahāyāna mind is the Bodhisattva's pure land, for when he attains Buddhahood all living beings seeking Mahāyāna will be reborn there.

"Charity (dāna) is the Bodhisattva's pure land, for when he attains Buddhahood living beings who can give away (to charity) will be reborn there.

"Discipline (śīla) is the Bodhisattva's pure land, for when he realizes Buddhahood living beings who have kept the ten prohibitions will be reborn there.

"Patience (kṣānti) is the Bodhisattva's pure land, for when he attains Buddhahood living beings endowed with the thirty-two excellent physical marks will be reborn there.

"Devotion (vīrya) is the Bodhisattva's pure land, for when he attains Buddhahood living beings who are diligent in their performance of meritorious deeds will be reborn there.

"Serenity (dhyāna) is the Bodhisattva's pure land, for when he attains Buddhahood living beings whose minds are disciplined and unstirred will be reborn there.

"Wisdom (prajñā) is the Bodhisattva's pure land, for when he attains Buddhahood living beings who have realized samādhi will be reborn there.

"The four boundless minds (catvāri apramāṇāni)[1] are the Bodhisattva's pure land, for when he attains Buddhahood living beings who have practised and perfected the four infinites: kindness, compassion, joy and indifference, will be reborn there.

"The four persuasive actions (catuḥ-saṁgraha-vastu)[2] are the Bodhisattva's pure land, for when he attains Buddhahood living beings who have benefited from his helpful persuasion will be reborn there.

"The expedient methods (upāya)[3] of teaching the absolute truth are the Bodhisattva's pure land, for when he attains Buddhahood living beings conversant with upāya will be reborn there.

"The thirty-seven contributory states to enlightenment (bodhipākṣika-dharma)[4] are the Bodhisattva's pure land, for when he attains Buddhahood living beings who have successfully practised the four states of mindfulness (smṛtyupasthāna),[5] the four proper lines of exertion (samyakpra-

[1] Catvāri apramāṇāni, the four immeasurables, or infinite Buddha states of mind: boundless kindness (maitrī), bestowing of joy and happiness; boundless compassion (karuṇā) to save from suffering; boundless joy (muditā) on seeing others rescued from suffering; and limitless indifference (upekṣā) i.e. rising above these emotions, or giving up all things such as distinction of friend and enemy, etc., thus wiping out all discrimination.

[2] Catuḥ-saṁgraha-vastu, the four Bodhisattva winning actions: (*a*) dāna, giving what others like in order to lead them to love and receive the truth; (*b*) priyavacana, affectionate speech, with the same purpose; (*c*) arthakṛtya, conduct profitable to others with the same purpose; and (*d*) samānārthatā, cooperation with and adaptation of oneself to others to lead them into the truth.

[3] Upāya: skilful expedient methods of expounding the inexpressible and indescribable absolute state of enlightenment.

[4] The thirty-seven stages contributory to enlightenment (bodhipākṣika-dharma): the four stages of mindfulness, the four proper lines of exertion, the four steps towards supramundane powers, the five spiritual faculties, the five transcendental powers, the seven degrees of enlightenment and the eightfold noble path.

[5] Smṛtyupasthāna: the fourfold stage of mindfulness that performs the fivefold Hīnayāna procedure for quieting the mind and consists of

hāṇa),[1] the four steps towards supramundane powers (ṛddhipāda),[2] the five spiritual faculties (pañca indriyāṇi),[3] the five transcendental powers (pañca balāni),[4] the seven degrees of enlightenment (sapta bodhyaṅga)[5] and the eightfold noble path (aṣṭa-mārga)[6] will be reborn in his land.

"Dedication (of one's merits to the salvation of others) is the Bodhisattva's pure land, for when he attains Buddhahood his land will be adorned with all kinds of meritorious virtues.

"Preaching the ending of the eight sad conditions[7] is the Bodhisattva's pure land, for when he attains Buddhahood his land will be free from these evil states.

---

contemplating: (*a*) the body as impure; (*b*) sensation as always resulting in suffering; (*c*) mind as impermanent; and (*d*) things as being dependent and without a nature of their own.

The fivefold Hīnayāna procedure to rid the mind of desire, hate, delusion, selfishness and confusion consists of meditation on impurity, compassion, causality, impartiality and counting the breaths.

[1] Samyakprahāṇa, the four right efforts: to put an end to existing evils; prevent evil arising; bring good into existence; and develop existing good.

[2] Ṛddhipāda, the four steps to ṛddhi or supernatural powers: intensive concentration, intensified effort, intense holding on to the position reached and intensified meditation on the underlying principle.

[3] Pañca-indriyāṇi, the five spiritual faculties: faith, devotion, right thought, concentration and wisdom.

[4] Pañca-balāni, the five powers of faith, destroying doubt; devotion, destroying remissness; right thought, destroying falsity; concentration, destroying confused and wandering thoughts; and wisdom, destroying ignorance.

[5] Sapta-bodhyaṅga, the seven degrees of enlightenment: discerning the true and the false; zeal; delight; weightlessness; right mindfulness; serenity; and indifference to all states.

[6] Aṣṭa-mārga, the eightfold noble path: correct views, correct thought, correct speech, correct conduct, correct livelihood, correct efforts, correct mindfulness and correct meditation.

[7] The eight sad conditions in which it is difficult to meet a Buddha or hear his Dharma: in the hells; as hungry ghosts; as animals; in Uttarakuru, the northern world where all is pleasant and people have no chance to hear about the Dharma; in the long-life heavens, where life is long and easy and where people never think of the Dharma; as deaf, blind and dumb; as a worldly philosopher who despises the Dharma; and in the intermediate period between a Buddha and his successor.

"To keep the precepts while refraining from criticizing those who do not is the Bodhisattva's pure land, for when he attains Buddhahood his country will be free from people who break the commandments.

"The ten good deeds[1] are the Bodhisattva's pure land, for when he attains Buddhahood he will not die young,[2] he will be wealthy,[3] he will live purely,[4] his words are true,[5] his speech is gentle,[6] his entourage will not desert him because of his conciliatoriness,[7] his talk is profitable to others,[8] and living beings free from envy and anger and holding right views will be reborn in his land.

"So, Ratna-rāśi, because of his straightforward mind, a Bodhisattva can act straightforwardly; because of his straightforward deeds he realizes the profound mind; because of his profound mind his thoughts are kept under control; because of his controlled thoughts his acts accord with the Dharma (he has heard); because of his deeds in accord with the Dharma he can dedicate his merits to the benefit of others; because of this dedication he can make use of expedient methods (upāya); because of his expedient methods he can bring living beings to perfection; because he can bring them to perfection his Buddha land is pure; because of his pure Buddha land his preaching of the Dharma is pure; because of his pure preaching his wisdom is pure; because of his pure wisdom his mind

[1] i.e. the non-committal of the ten evils: killing, stealing, carnality, lying, double tongue, coarse language, affected speech, desire, anger and perverse views.

[2] Because he refrains from killing.

[3] Because he refrains from stealing.

[4] Because he refrains from carnality.

[5] Because he does not lie.

[6] Because he refrains from coarse language.

[7] Because he refrains from double tongue.

[8] Because he avoids affected speech.

is pure, and because of his pure mind all his merits are pure.

"Therefore, Ratna-rāśi, if a Bodhisattva wants to win the pure land he should purify his mind, and because of his pure mind the Buddha land is pure."

As Śāriputra was fascinated by the Buddha's awe-inspiring majesty, he thought: "If the Buddha land is pure because of the Bodhisattva's pure mind, is it because the mind of the World Honoured One was not pure when He was still in the Bodhisattva stage, that this Buddha land (i.e. this world) is so unclean (as we see it now)?"

The Buddha knew of his thought and said to Śāriputra: "Are the sun and the moon not clean when a blind man does not see their cleanliness?" Śāriputra said: "World Honoured One, this is the fault of the blind man and not that of the sun and the moon." The Buddha said: "Śāriputra, because of their (spiritual) blindness living beings do not see the imposing majesty of the Tathāgata's pure land; this is not the fault of the Tathāgata. Śāriputra, this land of mine is pure but you do not see its purity."

Thereupon, Brahmā with a tuft of hair on his head (resembling a conch) said to Śāriputra: "Don't think this Buddha land is impure. Why? Because I see that the land of Śākyamuni Buddha is pure and clean, like a heavenly palace." Śāriputra said: "I see that this world is full of hills, mountains, pits, thorns, stones and earth, which are all unclean." Brahmā said: "Because your mind is up and down and disagrees with the Buddha-wisdom, you see that this land is unclean. Śāriputra, because a Bodhisattva is impartial towards all living beings and his profound mind is pure and clean in accord with the Buddha Dharma, he can see that this Buddha land is (also) pure and clean."

Thereat, the Buddha pressed the toes of His (right) foot

on the ground and the world was suddenly adorned with hundreds and thousands of rare and precious gems of the great chiliocosm, like the Precious Majestic Buddha's pure land adorned with countless precious merits which the assembly praised as never seen before; in addition each person present found himself seated on a precious lotus throne.

The Buddha said to Śāriputra: "Look at the majestic purity of this Buddha land of mine." Śāriputra said: "World Honoured One, I have never seen and heard of this Buddha land in its majestic purity." The Buddha said: "This Buddha land of mine is always pure, but appears filthy so that I can lead people of inferior spirituality to their salvation. This is like the food of devas which takes various colours according to the merits of each individual eater. So, Śāriputra, the man whose mind is pure sees this world in its majestic purity."

When this Buddha land (i.e. the world) appeared in its majestic purity the five hundred sons of elders who came with Ratna-rāśi, realized the patient endurance of the uncreate (anutpattika-dharma-kṣānti), and eighty-four thousand people developed their minds set on Supreme Enlightenment (anuttara-samyak-saṁbodhi).

The Buddha then stopped pressing His toes on the ground and the world returned to its previous (filthy) condition. Thirty-two thousand devas and men aspiring to the śrāvaka stage, understood the impermanence of all phenomena, kept from earthly impurities and achieved the Dharma-eye (which sees the truth of the four noble truths),[1] eight thousand bhikṣus kept from phenomena and succeeded in putting an end to the stream of transmigration (thus realizing arhatship).

[1] The four noble truths (catvāriārya-satyāni) are: suffering (duḥkha), its cause (samudāya), its ending (nirodha) and the way thereto (mārga). They were first preached by the Buddha to His five former ascetic companions and those who accepted them were in the śrāvaka stage.

CHAPTER TWO

The Expedient Method (upāya) of Teaching

IN the great town of Vaiśālī there was an elder called Vimalakīrti who had made offerings to countless Buddhas and had deeply planted all good roots, thereby achieving the patient endurance of the uncreate. His unhindered power of speech enabled him to roam everywhere using his supernatural powers to teach others. He had achieved absolute control over good and evil influences (dhāraṇī) thereby realizing fearlessness. So he overcame all passions and demons, entered all profound Dharma-doors to enlightenment, excelled in Wisdom perfection (prajñā-pāramitā) and was well versed in all expedient methods (upāya)[1] of teaching, thereby fulfilling all great Bodhisattva vows.[2] He knew very well the mental propensities of living beings and could distinguish their various (spiritual) roots. For a long time he had trodden the Buddha-path and his mind was spotless. Since he understood Mahāyāna, all his actions were based on right thinking. While dwelling in the Buddha's awe-inspiring majesty, his mind was extensive like the great ocean. He was praised by all Buddhas and revered by Indra and Brahmā. As he was set on saving men, he expediently stayed at Vaiśālī for this purpose.

He used his unlimited wealth to aid the poor;[3] he kept all

[1] Upāya, expedient method to teach and explain the inconceivable and inexpressible absolute state of enlightenment.

[2] e.g. the forty-eight great vows of Amitābha Buddha. See *The Secrets of Chinese Meditation*, p. 81. (Rider, London; Weiser, New York.)

[3] His practice of dāna-pāramitā or charity-perfection.

the rules of morality and discipline to correct those breaking the precepts;[1] he used his great patience to teach those giving rise to anger and hate;[2] he taught zeal and devotion to those who were remiss;[3] he used serenity to check stirring thoughts;[4] and employed decisive wisdom to defeat ignorance.[5] Although wearing white clothes (of the laity) he observed all the rules of the Saṅgha. Although a layman, he was free from all attachments to the three worlds (of desire, form and beyond form). Although he was married and had children, he was diligent in his practice of pure living. Although a householder, he delighted in keeping from domestic establishments. Although wearing jewels and ornaments, he embellished his body with its majestic spiritual characteristics.[6] Although he ate and drank (like others), he delighted in tasting the flavour of meditation.[7] When entering a gambling house he always tried to teach and deliver people there. He received heretics but never strayed from the right faith. Though he knew worldly classics, he always took joy in the Buddha Dharma. He was revered by all who met him. He upheld the right Dharma and taught it to old and young people.

Although occasionally he realized some profit in his worldly activities, he was not happy about these earnings. While walking in the street he never failed to convert others (to the Dharma). When he entered a government office, he always protected others (from injustice). When joining a symposium he led others to the Mahāyāna. When visiting a

[1] His practice of śīla-pāramitā or discipline-perfection.

[2] His practice of kṣānti-pāramitā or patience-perfection.

[3] His practice of vīrya-pāramitā or zeal-perfection.

[4] His practice of dhyāna-pāramitā or meditation-perfection.

[5] His practice of prajñā-pāramitā or wisdom-perfection.

[6] Spiritual characteristics as revealed by his right practice of the Dharma.

[7] i.e. the mysterious taste or sensation experienced by one who achieves serenity or dhyāna.

school he enlightened the students. When entering a house of prostitution he revealed the sin of sexual intercourse. When going to a tavern, he stuck to his determination (to abstain from drinking). When amongst elders he was the most revered for he taught them the exalted Dharma. When amongst upāsakas[1] he was the most respected for he taught them how to wipe out all desires and attachments. When amongst those of the ruling class, he was the most revered for he taught them forbearance. When amongst Brahmins, he was the most revered for he taught them how to conquer pride and prejudice. When amongst government officials he was the most revered for he taught them correct law. When amongst princes, he was the most revered for he taught them loyalty and filial piety. When in the inner palaces, he was the most revered for he converted all maids of honour there. When amongst common people, he was the most revered for he urged them to cultivate all meritorious virtues. When amongst Brahma-devas, he was the most revered for he urged the gods to realize the Buddha wisdom. When amongst Śakras and Indras, he was the most revered for he revealed to them the impermanence (of all things). When amongst lokapālas,[2] he was the most revered for he protected all living beings.

Thus Vimalakīrti used countless expedient methods (upāya) to teach for the benefit of living beings. Now using upāya he appeared ill, and because of his indisposition kings, ministers, elders, upāsakas, Brahmins, etc., as well as princes and other officials numbering many thousands came to enquire after his health.

So Vimalakīrti appeared in his sick body to receive and expound the Dharma to them, saying: "Virtuous ones, the human body is impermanent; it is neither strong nor

[1] Upāsaka, a male devotee who remains in the world as a lay disciple.
[2] The guardians of the world and of the Dharma.

durable; it will decay and is, therefore, unreliable. It causes anxieties and sufferings, being subject to all kinds of ailments. Virtuous ones, all wise men do not rely on this body which is like a mass of foam, which is intangible. It is like a bubble and does not last for a long time. It is like a flame and is the product of the thirst of love. It is like a banana tree, the centre of which is hollow. It is like an illusion being produced by inverted thoughts. It is like a dream being formed by false views. It is like a shadow and is caused by karma. This body is like an echo for it results from causes and conditions. It is like a floating cloud which disperses any moment. It is like lightning for it does not stay for the time of a thought. It is ownerless for it is like the earth. It is egoless for it is like fire (that kills itself). It is transient like the wind. It is not human for it is like water. It is unreal and depends on the four elements for its existence. It is empty, being neither ego nor its object. It is without knowledge like grass, trees and potsherds. It is not the prime mover, but is moved by the wind (of passions). It is impure and full of filth. It is false, and though washed, bathed, clothed and fed, it will decay and die in the end. It is a calamity being subject to all kinds of illnesses and sufferings. It is like a dry well for it is pursued by death. It is unsettled and will pass away. It is like a poisonous snake, a deadly enemy, a temporary assemblage (without underlying reality), being made of the five aggregates, the twelve entrances (the six organs and their objects) and the eighteen realms of sense (the six organs, their objects and their perceptions).

"Virtuous ones, the (human) body being so repulsive, you should seek the Buddha body. Why? Because the Buddha body is called Dharmakāya,[1] the product of boundless

[1] i.e. the essential spiritual body of the Buddha, free from birth and death; it is formless and beyond the three realms of desire, form and formlessness.

merits and wisdom; the outcome of discipline, meditation, wisdom, liberation and perfect knowledge of liberation; the result of kindness, compassion, joy and indifference (to emotions); the consequence of (the six perfections or pāramitās:) charity, discipline, patience, zeal, meditation and wisdom, and the sequel of expedient teaching (upāya); the six supernatural powers;[1] the three insights;[2] the thirty-seven stages contributory to enlightenment;[3] serenity and insight;[4] the ten transcendental powers (daśabala);[5] the four kinds of fearlessness;[6] the eighteen unsurpassed characteristics of the Buddha;[7] the wiping out of all evils and the performance of all good deeds; truthfulness, and freedom from looseness and unrestraint.

"So countless kinds of purity and cleanness produce the body of the Tathāgata. Virtuous ones, if you want to realize the Buddha body in order to get rid of all the illnesses of a living being, you should set your minds on the quest of supreme enlightenment (anuttara-samyak-saṁbodhi)."

Thus the elder Vimalakīrti expounded the Dharma to all those who came to enquire after his health, urging countless visitors to seek supreme enlightenment.

[1] The six supernatural powers (ṣaḍabhijñā): 1, divine sight, 2, divine hearing; 3, knowledge of the minds of all living beings; 4, knowledge of all forms of previous existences of self and others; 5, power to appear at will in any place and to have absolute freedom; and 6, insight into the ending of the stream of birth and death.

[2] The three insights into the mortal conditions of self and others in previous lives; future mortal conditions; and present mortal sufferings so as to overcome all passions and temptations.

[3] The thirty-seven contributory conditions of enlightenment, see p. 10, nn. 4-5 and p. 11, nn. 1-6.

[4] i.e. śamatha-vipaśyanā or chih kuan, see *The Secrets of Chinese Meditation*, pp. 109-162. (Rider, London; Weiser, New York.)

[5] Daśabala, see p. 2, n. 1.

[6] The four kinds of Buddha fearlessness arise from his omniscience; perfection of character; overcoming opposition; and ending of suffering.

[7] The eighteen unsurpassed characteristics of a Buddha, see p. 3, n. 1.

CHAPTER THREE

The Disciples

VIMALAKĪRTI wondered why the great compassionate Buddha did not take pity on him as he was confined to bed suffering from an indisposition. The Buddha knew of his thought and said to Śāriputra: "Go to Vimalakīrti to enquire after his health on my behalf."

Śāriputra said: "World Honoured One, I am not qualified to call on him and enquire after his health. The reason is that once, as I was sitting in meditation under a tree in a grove, Vimalakīrti came and said: 'Śāriputra, meditation is not necessarily sitting. For meditation means the non-appearance of body and mind in the three worlds (of desire, form and no form); giving no thought to inactivity when in nirvāṇa while appearing (in the world) with respect-inspiring deportment;[1] not straying from the Truth while attending to worldly affairs; the mind abiding neither within nor without; being imperturbable to wrong views during the practice of the thirty-seven contributory stages leading to enlightenment:[2] and not wiping out troubles (kleśa) while entering the state of nirvāṇa. If you can thus sit in meditation, you will win the Buddha's seal.'

"World Honoured One, when I heard his speech I was dumbfounded and found no word to answer him. Therefore

[1] Perfect passivity in nirvāṇa is useless if a Bodhisattva neglects his work of salvation.

[2] The thirty-seven states contributory to enlightenment, see p. 10, nn. 4-5 and p. 11, nn. 1-6.

I am not qualified to call on him and enquire after his health."

The Buddha then said to Maudgalaputra: "Go to Vimalakīrti and enquire after his health on my behalf."

Maudgalaputra said: "World Honoured One, I am not qualified to call on him to enquire after his health. The reason is that one day when I came to Vaiśālī to expound the Dharma to lay Buddhists (upāsakas) in the street there, Vimalakīrti came and said: 'Hey, Maudgalaputra, when expounding the Dharma to these upāsakas, you should not preach like that for what you teach should agree with the absolute Dharma which is free from the (illusion of) living beings;[1] is free from the self for it is beyond an ego;[1] from life for it is beyond birth and death[1] and from the concept of a man which lacks continuity (though seemingly continuous, like a torch whirled around);[1] is always still for it is beyond (stirring) phenomena; is above form for it is causeless; is inexpressible for it is beyond word and speech; is inexplainable for it is beyond intellection; is formless like empty space; is beyond sophistry for it is immaterial; is egoless for it is beyond (the duality of) subject and object; is free from discrimination for it is beyond consciousness; is without compare for it is beyond all relativities; is beyond cause for it is causeless; is identical with Dharmatā (or Dharma-nature), the underlying nature (of all things); is in line with the

[1] Vimalakīrti knew that the audience was of very high spirituality and should be taught the absolute reality. Maudgalaputra, however, followed the Hīnayāna practice to teach them the precepts which ensured their rebirth in heavens thereby giving rise to the idea of devas or living beings enjoying blessedness there, followed by discriminatory views which would hinder their realization of absolute bodhi.

Vimalakīrti referred to the four illusions of ego, man, living being and life as expounded by the Buddha in the Diamond Sūtra. See Ch'an and Zen Teaching, Series One, *The Diamond Cutter of Doubts*, pp. 147-206. (Rider, London; Shambala, Berkeley.)

absolute for it is independent; dwells in the region of absolute reality, being above and beyond all dualities; is unmovable for it does not rely on the six objects of sense; neither comes nor goes for it does not stay anywhere; is in line with voidness, formlessness and inactivity;[1] is beyond beauty and ugliness; neither increases nor decreases; is beyond creation and destruction; does not return to anywhere; is above the six sense organs of eye, ear, nose, tongue, body and mind; is neither up nor down; is eternal and immutable; and is beyond contemplation and practice.

" 'Maudgalaputra, such being the characteristics of the Dharma, how can it be expounded? For expounding it is beyond speech and indication, and listening to it is above hearing and grasping. This is like a conjurer expounding the Dharma to illusory men, and you should always bear all this in mind when expounding the Dharma. You should be clear about the sharp or dull roots of your audience and have a good knowledge of this to avoid all sorts of hindrance. Before expounding the Dharma you should use your great compassion (for all living beings) to extoll Mahāyāna to them, and think of repaying your (own) debt of gratitude to the Buddha by striving to preserve the three treasures (of Buddha, Dharma and Saṅgha) for ever.'

"When Vimalakīrti spoke, eight hundred upāsakas set their minds on seeking supreme enlightenment (anuttara-samyak-saṁbodhi). I do not have the eloquence and am, therefore, not fit to call on him to enquire after his health."

The Buddha then said to Mahākāśyapa: "Go to Vimalakīrti to enquire after his health on my behalf."

Mahākāśyapa said: "World Honoured One, I am not

[1] The three gates to nirvāṇa are voidness, formlessness and inactivity.

qualified to call on him to enquire after his health. The reason is that once when I went begging for food in a lane inhabited by poor people, Vimalakīrti came and said: 'Hey, Mahākāśyapa, you are failing to make your kind and compassionate mind all-embracing by begging from the poor while staying away from the rich.

" 'Mahākāśyapa, in your practice of impartiality you should call on your donors in succession (regardless of whether they are poor or rich). You should beg for food without the (ulterior) idea of eating it. To wipe out the concept of rolling (food into a ball in the hand)[1] you should take it by the hand (i.e. without the idea of how you take it). You should receive the food given without the idea of receiving anything. When entering a village you should regard it as void like empty space. When seeing a form you should remain indifferent to it. When you hear a voice you should consider it (as meaningless as) an echo. When you smell an odour take it for the wind (which has no smell). When you eat, refrain from discerning the taste. Regard all touch as if you were realizing wisdom (which is free from feelings and emotions). You should know that all things are illusory, having neither nature of their own nor that of something else, and that since fundamentally they are not self-existent they cannot now be the subject of annihilation.

" 'Mahākāśyapa, if you can achieve all eight forms of

[1] There are four kinds of food: (*a*) that eaten in the Indian way by first rolling the food into a ball in the hand and then bringing it to the mouth to nourish the body and preserve life; (*b*) vow-food derived from the practiser's vow that develops all good roots inherent in him; (*c*) karmic food that sustains the lives of sufferers in the hells; and (*d*) spiritual food by which devas in the formless realms are kept alive. The text means that eating should be free from all attachment to food in order to be in line with absolute reality.

liberation[1] without keeping from the eight heterodox ways (of life),[2] that is by identifying heterodoxy with orthodoxy (both as emanating from the same source), and if you can make an offering of your (own) food to all living beings as well as to all Buddhas and all members of the Saṅgha, then you can take the food. Such a way of eating is beyond the troubles (of the worldly man) and the absence of the troubles of Hīnayāna men); above the state of stillness (in which Hīnayāna men abstain from eating) and the absence of stillness (of Mahāyāna men who eat while in the state of serenity); and beyond both dwelling in the worldly state or in nirvāṇa, while your donors reap neither great nor little merits, what they give being neither beneficial nor harmful. This is correct entry upon the Buddha path without relying on the small way of śrāvakas. Mahākāśyapa, if you can so eat the food given you, your eating shall not be in vain.'

"World Honoured One, when I listened to his words which I had never heard before, I gave rise to profound reverence to all Bodhisattvas and thought, 'His wisdom and power of speech being such, who will fail to develop a mind set on supreme enlightenment?' Since then I have refrained from urging people to follow the practices of śrāvakas and

[1] Liberation in eight forms (aṣṭa-vimokṣa): 1, liberation, when subjective desire arises, by examination of the object, or of all things and realization of their filthiness; 2, liberation, when no subjective desire arises, by still meditation as above; 3, liberation by concentration on the pure to the realization of a permanent state of freedom from all desires; 4, liberation in realizing the infinity of space, or the immaterial; 5, liberation in realizing infinite knowledge; 6, liberation in realizing nothingness; 7, liberation in the state of mind where there is neither thought nor absence of thought; and 8, liberation by means of a state of mind in which there is final extinction of both sensation (vedanā) and conception (sañjñā). 1 and 2 are deliverance by meditating on impurity, and 3 on purity.

[2] The opposite of the eightfold noble path: 1, wrong views; 2, wrong thoughts; 3, false and idle talk; 4, heterodox conduct; 5, heterodox livelihood or occupation; 6, false zeal; 7, wrong mindfulness; and 8, heterodox meditation.

pratyeka-buddhas. Hence I am not qualified to call on him to enquire after his health."

The Buddha then said to Subhūti: "You call on Vimalakīrti to enquire after his health on my behalf."

Subhūti said: "World Honoured One, I am not qualified to call on him and enquire after his health. The reason is that once when I went to his house begging for food, he took my bowl and filled it with rice, saying: 'Subhūti, if your mind set on eating is in the same state as when confronting all (other) things, and if this uniformity as regards all things equally applies to (the act of) eating, you can then beg for food and eat it. Subhūti, if without cutting off carnality, anger and stupidity you can keep from these (three) evils:[1] if you do not wait for the death of your body to achieve the oneness of all things; if you do not wipe out stupidity and love in your quest of enlightenment and liberation;[2] if you can look into (the underlying nature of) the five deadly sins[3] to win liberation, with at the same time no idea of either bondage or freedom; if you give rise to neither the four noble truths[4] nor their opposites; if you do not hold both the concept of winning and not winning the holy fruit; if you do not regard yourself as a worldly or unworldly man, as a saint or not as a saint; if you perfect all Dharmas while

[1] The worldly man gives rise to carnality, anger and stupidity in his quest of earthly pleasures, and the śrāvakas cut off these three evils in their quest of relative nirvāṇa, but the Bodhisattva does not cut them off but merely refrains from giving rise to them in order to be free from dualities, relativities and contraries in his quest of absolute bodhi.

[2] The śrāvaka wipes out stupidity which screens his wisdom in order to realize enlightenment, and puts an end to love which keeps him in bondage to achieve liberation, but the Bodhisattva looks straight into the underlying nature of stupidity and love to eliminate all dualities, relativities and contraries to realize the absolute state of true enlightenment and true liberation.

[3] Parricide, matricide, killing an arhat, shedding the blood of a Buddha and destroying the harmony of the Saṅgha.

[4] The four noble truths, see p. 14, n. 1.

keeping away from the concept of Dharmas, then can you receive and eat the food. Subhūti, if you neither see the Buddha nor hear the Dharma; if the six heterodox teachers, Pūraṇa-kāśyapa, Maskari-gośālīputra, Sañjaya-vairāṭīputra, Ajita-keśakambala, Kakuda-kātyāyana and Nirgrantha-jñātiputra[1] are regarded impartially as your own teachers and if, when they induce leavers of home into heterodoxy, you also fall with the latter; then you can take away the food and eat it. If you are (unprejudiced about) falling into heresy and regard yourself as not reaching the other shore (of enlightenment); if you (are unprejudiced about) the eight sad conditions[2] and regard yourself as not free from them; if you (are unprejudiced about) defilements and relinquish the concept of pure living; if when you realize samādhi in which there is absence of debate or disputation, all living beings also achieve it; if your donors of food are not regarded (with partiality) as (cultivating) the field of blessedness; if those making offerings to you (are impartially looked on as also) falling into the three evil realms of existence; if you (impartially) regard demons as your companions without differentiating between them as well as between other forms of defilement; if you are discontented with all living beings,

[1] The six tīrthyas or heterodox teachers who were opponents of the Buddha: (*a*) Pūraṇa-kāśyapa who taught the non-existence of all things, that all was illusion, and that there was neither birth nor death therefore, neither prince nor subject, parent nor child, nor their duties; (*b*) Maskari-gośālīputra who denied that one's present lot was due to deeds done in previous lives; (*c*) Sañjaya-vairāṭīputra who taught that there was no need to seek the truth because when the necessary aeons have passed, mortality ends and happiness naturally follows; (*d*) Ajita-keśakambala whose cloak was his hair, and who was given to extravagant austerities; his doctrine was that happiness in the next life is correlative to the suffering of this life; (*e*) Kakuda-kātyāyana whose views changed according to circumstances; he replied "is" to those asking about existence and "is not" to those asking about non-existence; and (*f*) Nirgrantha-jñātiputra whose doctrines were determinist, everything being fated so that no religious practices could change one's lot.

[2] The eight sad conditions, see p. 11, n. 7.

defame the Buddha, break the law (Dharma), do not attain the holy rank, and fail to win liberation; then you can take away the food and eat it.'[1]

"World Honoured One, I was dumbfounded when I heard his words which were beyond my reach and to which I found no answer. Then I left the bowl of rice and intended to leave his house but Vimalakīrti said: 'Hey, Subhūti, take the bowl of rice without fear. Are you frightened when the Tathāgata makes an illusory man ask you questions?' I replied: 'No.' He then continued: 'All things are illusory and you should not fear anything. Why? Because words and speech are illusory. So all wise men do not cling to words and speech, and this is why they fear nothing. Why? Because words and speech have no independent nature of their own, and when they are no more, you are liberated. This liberation will free you from all bondage.'

"When Vimalakīrti expounded the Dharma two hundred sons of devas realized the Dharma eye.[2] Hence I am not qualified to call on him to enquire after his health."

The Buddha then said to Pūrṇamaitrāyaṇīputra: "You call on Vimalakīrti to enquire after his health on my behalf."

Pūrṇamaitrāyaṇīputra said: "World Honoured One, I am not qualified to call on him and enquire after his health. This is because when I was once in a grove and was expounding the Dharma under a tree to a group of newly initiated bhikṣus, Vimalakīrti came and said: 'Hey, Pūrṇamaitrāyaṇīputra, you should first enter the state of samādhi to examine the minds of your listeners before expounding the Dharma

1 Vimalakīrti taught Subhūti to cease differentiating and to remain indifferent to dualities, relativities and contraries so as to look into the underlying nature of all phenomena in order to develop an all-embracing mind in line with the oneness of absolute reality.

2 The Dharma eye is able to penetrate all things to see the truth that releases men from reincarnation.

to them. Do not put rotten food in precious bowls. You should know their minds and do not take their (precious) crystal for (ordinary) glass. If you do not know their propensities, do not teach them Hīnayāna. They have no wounds, so do not hurt them. To those who want to tread the wide path do not show narrow tracks. Do not enclose the great sea in the print of an ox's foot; do not liken sunlight to the dim glow of a firefly.'

" 'Pūrṇamaitrāyaṇīputra, these bhikṣus have long ago developed the Mahāyāna mind but they now forget all about it; how can you teach them Hīnayāna? Wisdom as taught by Hīnayāna is shallow; it is like a blind man who cannot discern the sharp from the dull roots of living beings.'

"Thereat, Vimalakīrti entered the state of samādhi and caused the bhikṣus to remember their former lives when they had met five hundred Buddhas and had then planted seeds of excellent virtues which they had dedicated to their quest of supreme enlightenment; they instantly awakened to their past and recovered their fundamental minds. They at once bowed with their heads at the feet of Vimalakīrti who then expounded the Dharma to them; they resumed their quest of supreme enlightenment without backsliding.

"I think that śrāvakas who do not know how to look into the roots of their listeners should not expound the Dharma. Hence I am not qualified to call on Vimalakīrti to enquire after his health."

The Buddha then said to Mahākātyāyana: "You go to Vimalakīrti to enquire after his health on my behalf."

Mahākātyāyana said: "World Honoured One, I am not qualified to call on him and enquire after his health. For once after the Buddha had expounded the essentials of the Dharma to a group of bhikṣus, I followed Him to explain to them the meanings of impermanence, suffering, voidness, egolessness and nirvāṇa.

"Vimalakīrti came and said: 'Hey, Mahākātyāyana, do not use your mortal mind to preach immortal reality. Mahākātyāyana, all things are fundamentally above creation and destruction; this is what impermanence means. The five aggregates are perceived as void and not arising; this is what suffering means. All things are basically non-existent; this is what voidness means. Ego and its absence are not a duality; this is what egolessness means. All things basically are not what they seem to be, they cannot be subject to extinction now; this is what nirvāṇa means.[1]

"After Vimalakīrti had expounded the Dharma, the bhikṣus present (succeeded in) liberating their minds. Hence I am not qualified to call on him and enquire after his health."

The Buddha then said to Aniruddha:[2] "You call on Vimalakīrti to enquire after his health on my behalf."

Aniruddha said: "World Honoured One, I am not qualified to call on him and enquire after his health. For once when I

[1] The Buddha teaches His disciples not to give rise to dualities, relativities and contraries, which are all false in order to realize absolute reality. Since worldly men cling to permanence, pleasure, reality, ego and existence, the Buddha speaks of their opposites to show the mutual dependence of the two extremes which have no independent nature, but He does not teach them to cling to impermanence, suffering, voidness, egolessness and nirvāṇa.

Mahākātyāyana did not understand the Buddha's profound teaching and in his talk to the bhikṣus, he clung to names and forms (nāma-rūpa) such as impermanance, suffering, voidness, egolessness and nirvāṇa; hence his errors which Vimalakīrti pointed out for correction.

Readers are referred to the Sixth Patriarch's Last Instructions (see Ch'an and Zen Teaching, third series, part 1, *The Altar Sūtra of the Sixth Patriarch*, p. 91. Rider, London; Shambala, Berkeley) in which Hui Neng teaches his disciples to deal with the mutual dependence of the two extremes of all dualities in order to bring to light the significance of the "mean" which is the aim of Mahāyāna.

[2] Aniruddha was one of the chief disciples of the Buddha; he was considered supreme in deva sight, or unlimited vision.

was walking about (while meditating to prevent sleepiness) a Brahmā called 'The Gloriously Pure' together with an entourage of ten thousand devas sent off rays of light, came to my place, bowed their heads to salute me and asked: 'How far does your deva eye see?' I replied: 'Virtuous one, I see the land of Śākyamuni Buddha in the great chiliocosm like an amala fruit[1] held in my hand.' Vimalakīrti (suddenly) came and said: 'Hey, Aniruddha, when your deva eye sees, does it see form or formlessness? If it sees form, you are no better than those heretics who have won five supernatural powers. If you see formlessness, your deva eye is non-active (wu wei) and should be unseeing.'

"World Honoured One, I kept silent and the devas praised Vimalakīrti for what they had not heard before. They then paid reverence and asked him: 'Is there anyone in this world who has realized the real deva eye?'[2] Vimalakīrti replied: 'There is the Buddha who has realized the real deva eye; He is always in the state of samādhi and sees all Buddha lands without (giving rise to) the duality (of subjective eye and objective form).'

"Thereat, Brahmā and five hundred of his relatives developed the anuttara-samyak-saṁbodhi mind; they bowed their heads at Vimalakīrti's feet and suddenly disappeared. This is why I am not qualified to call on him to enquire after his health."

The Buddha then said to Upāli: "You call on Vimalakīrti to enquire after his health on my behalf."

Upāli said: "World Honoured One, I am not qualified to call on Vimalakīrti to enquire after his health. For once, two bhikṣus broke the prohibitions, and being shameful of their

[1] A fruit like the betel nut, used as a cure for colds.

[2] Aniruddha did not achieve the real deva eye which cannot be screened by the illusion of form.

sins they dared not call on the Buddha. They came to ask me: 'Upāli, we have broken the commandments and are ashamed of our sins, so we dare not ask the Buddha about this and come to you. Please teach us the rules of repentance so as to wipe out our sins.' I then taught them the rules of repentance.

"Thereat Vimalakīrti came and said: 'Hey, Upāli, do not aggravate their sins which you should wipe out at once without further disturbing their minds. Why? Because the nature of sin is neither within nor without, nor in between.[1] As the Buddha has said, living beings are impure because their minds are impure; if their minds are pure they are all pure. And mind also is neither within nor without, nor in between.[2] Their minds being such, so are their sins. Likewise all things do not go beyond (their) suchness. Upāli, when your mind is liberated, is there any remaining impurity?' I replied: 'There will be no more.' He said: 'Likewise, the minds of all living beings are free from impurities. Upāli, false thoughts are impure and the absence of false thought is purity. Inverted (ideas) are impure and the absence of inverted (ideas) is purity. Clinging to ego is impure and non-clinging to ego is purity. Upāli, all phenomena rise and fall without staying (for an instant) like an illusion and lightning. All phenomena do not wait for one another and do not stay for the time of a thought. They all derive from false views and are like a dream and a flame, the moon in water, and an image in a mirror for they are born from wrong thinking. He who understands

1 Because sins have no independent nature of their own and are, therefore, non-existent. See also Ch'an and Zen Teaching, third series, part III, *The Song of Enlightenment*, p. 142. (Rider, London; Shambala, Berkeley.)

2 The mind is also non-existent and he who is clear about it, perceives his Buddha nature and attains Buddhahood, as Bodhidharma taught the Chinese after his arrival in China.

this is called a keeper of the rules of discipline and he who knows it is called a skilful interpreter (of the precepts).'

"Thereat the two bhikṣus declared: 'What a supreme wisdom which is beyond the reach of Upāli who cannot expound the highest principle of discipline and morality!' I said: 'Since I left the Buddha I have not met a śrāvaka or a Bodhisattva who can surpass his rhetoric for his great wisdom and perfect enlightenment have reached such a high degree.'

"Thereupon, the two bhikṣus got rid of their doubts and repentance,[1] set their minds on the quest of supreme enlightenment and took the vow to make all living beings acquire the same power of speech. Hence I am not qualified to call on Vimalakīrti and enquire after his health."

The Buddha then said to Rāhula: "You go to Vimalakīrti to enquire after his health on my behalf."

Rāhula said: "World Honoured One, I am not qualified to call on him and enquire after his health. For once the sons of the elders at Vaiśālī came to my place and bowed to salute me, saying: 'Rāhula, you are the Buddha's son and left the throne to search for the truth; what advantage derives from leaving home?' I then spoke of the advantage of earning merits that so derive. Vimalakīrti came and said: 'Hey, Rāhula, you should not speak of the advantage of earning merits that derive from leaving home. Why? Because home-leaving bestows neither advantage nor good merits. Only when speaking of the worldly (way of life) can you talk about advantage and merits. For home-leaving is above the worldly, and the transcendental is beyond advantage and merits. Rāhula, home-leaving is beyond thisness, thatness

[1] See also Ch'an and Zen Teaching, Series III, part II, *The Song of Enlightenment*, p. 114. (Rider, London; Shambala Berkeley.)

and in between; is above the sixty-two wrong views,[1] and abides in (the state of) nirvāṇa. It is praised by all wise men and practised by all saints. It overcomes all demons, liberates from the five realms of existence,[2] purifies the five kinds of eyes,[3] helps realize the five spiritual powers[4] and sets up the five spiritual faculties,[5] releases from earthly grievances, keeps from varied evils (derived from a mixed mind), frees from the unreality of names and terms, gets out of the mud (of defilement), relieves from all bondages, wipes out the duality of subject and object and all responsiveness and disturbances; it gives inner joy, protects all living beings, dwells in serenity and guards against all wrongs. If all this can be achieved, this is true home-leaving.'

"Vimalakīrti then said to the sons of the elders: 'During this period of correct Dharma[6] you should leave home to join the Saṅgha. Why? Because it is very difficult to have the good fortune of living in the Buddha-age.'[7] The sons of the elders replied: 'Venerable Upāsaka, we have heard the Buddha say that one cannot leave home without the consent

[1] The 62 views originate from the five aggregates which are considered under three periods of time. In the past each had permanence, impermanence, both or neither ($5 \times 4 = 20$). In the present, and here we deal with space or extension, each is finite, infinite, both or neither ($5 \times 4 = 20$). In the future each either continues or not, both or neither ($5 \times 4 = 20$), that is 60 in all. If the two ideas that body and mind are a unity or different are added, we have a total of 62.

[2] The five realms of existence: devas and asuras, men, animals, hungry ghosts and hells.

[3] The five kinds of eyes: the human eye, the deva eye or unlimited vision, the wisdom eye that sees all things as unreal, the Dharma eye, that penetrates all things, to see the truth that releases men from reincarnation, and the Buddha eye of the enlightened one who sees all and is omniscient.

[4] The five powers or pañca-balāni, see p. 11, n. 4.

[5] The five spiritual faculties or pañca-indriyāṇi, see p. 11, n. 3.

[6] The correct doctrine of the Buddha whose period was to last 500, some say 1,000 years, followed by the semblance period of 1,000 years, and then by the period of termination, lasting 10,000 years.

[7] The age when the Buddha was on earth.

of one's parents.' Vimalakīrti said: 'Yes, it is so, but you will really leave home the moment you develop a mind set on the quest of supreme enlightenment (anuttara-samyak-saṁbodhi) which completes your home-leaving.'

"Thereat, all the thirty-two sons of the elders developed the anuttara-samyak-saṁbodhi mind. This is why I am not qualified to call on Vimalakīrti and enquire after his health."

The Buddha then said to Ānanda: "You call on Vimalakīrti and enquire after his health on my behalf."

Ānanda replied: "World Honoured One, I am not qualified to call on him to enquire after his health. This is because once when the World Honoured One had a slight indisposition and needed some cow's milk, I took a bowl and went to a Brahmin family where I stood at the door. Vimalakīrti came and asked me: 'Why are you out so early holding a bowl in your hand?' I replied: 'Venerable Upāsaka, the World Honoured One is slightly indisposed and wants some cow's milk; this is why I have come here.' Vimalakīrti said: 'Stop, Ānanda, stop speaking these words. The Tathāgata's body is as strong as a diamond for He has cut off all evils and has achieved all good. What kind of indisposition and trouble does He still have? Ānanda, do not slander the Tathāgata and do not let other people hear such coarse language. Do not let the gods (devas) as well as the Bodhisattvas of other pure lands hear about it. Ānanda, a world ruler (cakravartī) who has accumulated only a few little merits is already free from all ailments; how much more so is the Tathāgata who has earned countless merits and has achieved all moral excellences? Go away, Ānanda, do not cover us all with shame. If the Brahmins heard you they would say: "How can this man be a saviour if he cannot cure his own illness; how can he pretend to heal the sick?" Get away unnoticed and quickly and do not let others hear what you have said. Ānanda, you should know that the body of the Tathāgata is the Dharmakāya and does not come from (the illusion of) thought and desire. The Buddha is the World Honoured One (Bhagavat); His body is above and beyond the three realms (of desire, form and beyond form) and is outside the stream of transmigratory suffering. The Buddha body is transcendental (wu wei) and is beyond destiny. How then can such a body be ill?'

"World Honoured One, his words covered me with shame and I asked myself if I had not wrongly understood the Buddha's order. Thereat, a voice was heard in the air above, saying: 'Ānanda, the upāsaka is right, but since the Buddha appears in the five kaṣāya (or periods of turbidity on earth),[1] He uses this (expedient) method (upāya) to liberate living beings. Ānanda, go and beg for the cow's milk without shame.'

"World Honoured One, Vimalakīrti's wisdom and power of speech being such, I am really not qualified to call on him to enquire after his health."

Thus each of the five hundred chief disciples related his encounter with Vimalakīrti and declined to call on him to enquire after his health.

[1] See *The Śūraṅgama Sūtra*, p. 105, n. 1 for detailed explanation of the five conditions of turbidity. (Rider, London.)

CHAPTER FOUR

The Bodhisattvas

THE Buddha then said to Maitreya Bodhisattva: "You go to Vimalakīrti to enquire after his health on my behalf."

Maitreya replied: "World Honoured One, I am not qualified to call on him and enquire after his health. The reason is that once when I was expounding to the deva-king and his retinue in the Tuṣita heaven the never-receding stage (of Bodhisattva development into Buddhahood) Vimalakīrti came and said to me: 'Maitreya, when the World Honoured One predicted your future attainment of supreme enlightenment (anuttara-samyak-saṁbodhi) in one lifetime, tell me in which life, whether in the past, future or present,[1] did or will you receive His prophecy? If it was in your past life, that has gone; if it will be in your future life, that has not yet come; and if it is in your present life, that does not stay. As the Buddha once said: 'O bhikṣus, you are born, are ageing and are dying simultaneously at this very moment'; if you received His prophecy in a lifeless (state), the latter is (precisely) the supreme stage in which there is neither prediction (of your future Buddhahood) nor realization of supreme enlightenment. How then did you receive the prediction of your attainment of Buddhahood in one lifetime? Or did you receive it in the absolute state (thatness or

[1] The three times (past, future and present) imply a duality of *is not* and *is*, the past which has gone and the future which has not yet come, standing for *is not* and the present which does not stay, but *is*. See also p. 122, n. 4 about the profound meaning of the sequence of the past, future and present in Mahāyāna texts.

tathatā) of either birth or death? If you receive it in the absolute state of birth, this absolute state is uncreated. If you receive it in the absolute state of death, this absolute state does not die. For (the underlying nature of) all living beings and of all things is absolute; all saints and sages are in this absolute state, and so also are you, Maitreya. So, if you, Maitreya, received the Buddha's prophecy of your future attainment of Buddhahood, all living beings (who are absolute by nature) should also receive it. Why? Because that which is absolute is non-dual and is beyond differentiation. If you, Maitreya, realize supreme enlightenment, so should all living beings. Why? Because they are the manifestation of bodhi (enlightenment). If you, Maitreya, win nirvāṇa, they should also realize it. Why? Because all Buddhas know that every living being is basically in the condition of extinction of existence and suffering which is nirvāṇa, in which there can be no further extinction of existence. Therefore, Maitreya, do not mislead the devas because there is neither development of supreme bodhi-mind nor its backsliding. Maitreya, you should instead urge them to keep from discriminating views about bodhi (enlightenment). Why? Because bodhi can be won by neither body nor mind. For bodhi is the state of calmness and extinction of passion (i.e. nirvāṇa) because it wipes out all forms. Bodhi is unseeing, for it keeps from all causes. Bodhi is non-discrimination, for it stops memorizing and thinking. Bodhi cuts off ideation, for it is free from all views. Bodhi forsakes inversion, for it prevents perverse thoughts. Bodhi puts an end to desire, for it keeps from longing. Bodhi is unresponsive, for it wipes out all clinging. Bodhi complies (with self-nature), for it is in line with the state of suchness. Bodhi dwells (in this suchness), for it abides in (changeless) Dharma-nature (or Dharmatā, the underlying nature of all things). Bodhi reaches this suchness, for it attains the region of reality. Bodhi is non-dual, for it keeps from (both) intellect and its objects. Bodhi is impartial, for it is equal to boundless space. Bodhi is the non-active (wu wei) state, for it is above the conditions of birth, existence and death. Bodhi is true knowledge, for it discerns the mental activities of all living beings. Bodhi does not unite, for it is free from all confrontation. Bodhi disentangles, for it breaks contact with habitual troubles (kleśa). Bodhi is that of which the position cannot be determined, for it is beyond form and shape, and is that which cannot be called by name for all names (have no independent nature and so) are void. Bodhi is like the mindlessness of an illusory man, for it neither accepts nor rejects anything. Bodhi is beyond disturbance, for it is always serene by itself. Bodhi is real stillness, because of its pure and clean nature. Bodhi is non-acceptance, for it keeps from causal attachments. Bodhi is non-differentiating, because of its impartiality towards all. Bodhi is without compare, for it is indescribable. Bodhi is profound and subtle, for although unknowing, it knows all.'

"World Honoured One, when Vimalakīrti so expounded the Dharma, two hundred sons of devas realized the patient endurance of the uncreate (anutpattika-dharma-kṣānti). This is why I am not qualified to call on him and enquire after his health."

The Buddha then said to the Bodhisattva Glorious Light: "You go to Vimalakīrti to enquire after his health on my behalf."

Glorious Light replied: "World Honoured One, I am not qualified to call on him to enquire after his health. The reason is that once while I was leaving Vaiśālī I met Vimalakīrti who was entering it. I saluted and asked him: 'Where does the Venerable Upāsaka come from?' He replied:

'From a bodhimaṇḍala (a holy site).'[1] I asked him: 'Where is this bodhimaṇḍala?' He replied: 'The straightforward mind is the bodhimaṇḍala, for it is free from falsehood. The initiated mind is the bodhimaṇḍala, for it can keep discipline. The profound mind is the bodhimaṇḍala, for it accumulates merits. The enlightened mind is the bodhimaṇḍala for it is infallible. Charity (dāna) is the bodhimaṇḍala, for it does not expect reward. Discipline (śīla) is the bodhimaṇḍala, for it fulfills all vows. Patience (kṣānti) is the bodhimaṇḍala for it has access to the minds of all living beings. Zeal (vīrya) is the bodhimaṇḍala, for it is free from remissness. Serenity (dhyāna) is the bodhimaṇḍala, because of its harmonious mind. Wisdom (prajñā) is the bodhimaṇḍala, for it discerns all things. Kindness (maitrī) is the bodhimaṇḍala, for it treats all living beings on an equal footing. Compassion (karuṇā) is the bodhimaṇḍala, because of its great forbearance. Joy (muditā) is the bodhimaṇḍala, for it is pleasant. Indifference (upekṣā) is the bodhimaṇḍala, for it wipes out both love and hate. Transcendental efficiency is the bodhimaṇḍala, for it perfects all the six supernatural powers (ṣaḍabhijñā).[2] Liberation is the bodhimaṇḍala, for it turns its back to all phenomenal conditions. Expedient devices (upāya) are the bodhimaṇḍala, for they teach and convert living beings. The four winning actions of a

[1] Bodhimaṇḍala, a circle, holy site or place of enlightenment; the place where the Buddha or a master attained bodhi; a place for realizing the Buddha truth; a place for teaching or learning the Dharma; a place where a Bodhisattva appears and where devotees have glimpses of him, for instance, Mount O Mei, in Western China, which is the bodhimaṇḍala of Samantabhadra Bodhisattva; Wu T'ai Shan, or the Five-Peaked Mountain in North China, that of Mañjuśrī; P'u T'o Island, off Ningpo, East China, that of Avalokiteśvara Bodhisattva, and Ts'ao Ch'i in Kuang Tung, South China, that of the Sixth Patriarch. A Monastery where a monk awakens to the Dharma is a bodhimaṇḍala.

[2] The six supernatural powers: see p. 19, n. 1.

Bodhisattva[1] are the bodhimaṇḍala, for they benefit all living beings. Wide knowledge through hearing the Dharma is the bodhimaṇḍala, for its practice leads to enlightenment. Control of the mind is the Bodhimaṇḍala, because of its correct perception of all things. The thirty-seven contributory stages to enlightenment[2] are the bodhimaṇḍala, for they keep from all worldly activities. The four noble truths[3] are the bodhimaṇḍala, because they do not deceive. The twelve links in the chain of existence[4] are the bodhimaṇḍala, because of their underlying nature which is infinite. Troubles (kleśa) are the bodhimaṇḍala, for their underlying nature is reality. Living beings are the bodhimaṇḍala, because they are (basically) egoless. All things are the bodhimaṇḍala, for they are empty. The defeat of demons is the bodhimaṇḍala, for it is imperturbable. The three realms (of desire, form and beyond form) are the bodhimaṇḍala, for fundamentally they lead to no real destination. The lion's roar is the bodhimaṇḍala, because of its fearlessness. The ten powers (daśabala),[5] the four kinds of fearlessness[6] and the eighteen unsurpassed characteristics of the Buddha[7] are the bodhi-

[1] The four Bodhisattva winning actions (catuḥ-saṁgraha-vastu), see p. 10, n. 2.

[2] The thirty-seven contributory conditions to enlightenment (saptatriṁśa-bodhipākṣikadharma), see p. 10, nn. 4-5 and p. 11, nn. 1-6.

[3] The four noble truths (catvāriārya-satyāni), see p. 14, n. 1.

[4] The twelve causes in the chain of existence (nidāna): from unenlightenment, dispositions; from dispositions, consciousness; from consciousness, name and form; from name and form, the six sense organs; from the six sense organs, contact; from contact, sensation; from sensation, desire; from desire, grasping; from grasping, becoming; from becoming, rebirth; and from rebirth, old age and death.

[5] The ten powers of a Buddha (daśabala), see p. 2, n. 1.

[6] The four kinds of fearlessness: Buddha's fearlessness arises from his omniscience; perfection of character; overcoming opposition; and ending suffering.

[7] The eighteen unsurpassed characteristics of a Buddha (āveṇikadharma), see p. 3, n. 1.

maṇḍala, for they are faultless. The three insights[1] are the bodhimaṇḍala, for they are free from all remaining hindrances. The knowledge of all things in the time of a thought is the bodhimaṇḍala, for it brings omniscience (sarvajña) to perfection. Thus, son of good family,[2] a Bodhisattva should convert living beings according to the various modes of perfection (pāramitās) and all his acts, including the raising or lowering of a foot,[3] should be interpreted as coming from the seat of learning (bodhimaṇḍala); he should thus stay within the Buddha Dharma.'

"While Vimalakīrti was thus expounding the Dharma, five hundred devas developed their minds set on supreme enlightenment. This is why I am not qualified to call on him to enquire after his health."

The Buddha then said to the Bodhisattva Ruler of the World: "You call on Vimalakīrti to enquire after his health on my behalf."

Ruler of the World replied: "World Honoured One, I am not qualified to call on him and enquire after his health. I still remember that once as I was staying in a vihāra, a demon like Indra appeared followed by twelve thousand goddesses (devakanyā) playing music and singing songs. After bowing their heads at my feet they brought their palms together and stood at my side. I mistook the demon for Śakra and said to him: 'Welcome, Śakra, although you have won merits, you should guard against passions (arising from music, song and sex). You should look into the five desires (for the objects of

[1] The three insights, see p. 19, n. 2.

[3] A conventional way of addressing a disciple of the Buddha.

[3] The functioning of a non-discriminating mind reveals the latter's perfection, and is frequently used by Ch'an masters to awaken their advanced disciples to the mind Dharma.

the five senses) in your practice of morality. You should look into the impermanence of body, life and wealth in your quest of indestructible Dharma (i.e. boundless body, endless life and inexhaustible spiritual wealth).'

"He said: 'Bodhisattva, please take these twelve thousand goddesses who will serve you.'

"I replied: 'Śakra, please do not make to a monk this unclean offering which does not suit me.'

"Even before I had finished speaking, Vimalakīrti came and said: 'He is not Śakra; he is a demon who comes to disturb you.' He then said to the demon: 'You can give me these girls and I will keep them.'

"The demon was frightened, and being afraid that Vimalakīrti might give him trouble, he tried to make himself invisible but failed, and in spite of his use of supernatural powers he could not go away. Suddenly a voice was heard in the air, saying: 'Demon, give him the girls and then you can go.' Being scared, he gave the girls to Vimalakīrti who said to them: 'The demon has given you to me. You can now develop a mind set on the quest of supreme enlightenment.'

"Vimalakīrti then expounded the Dharma to them urging them to seek the truth. He declared: 'You have now set your minds on the quest for the truth and can experience joy in the Dharma instead of in the five worldly pleasures (arising from the objects of the five senses).'

"They asked him: 'What is this joy in the Dharma?'

"He replied: 'Joy in having faith in the Buddha, joy in listening to the Dharma, joy in making offerings to the Saṅgha, and joy in forsaking the five worldly pleasures; joy in finding out that the five aggregates are like deadly enemies, that the four elements (that make the body) are like poisonous snakes, and that the sense organs and their objects are empty like space; joy in following and upholding the truth; joy in being beneficial to living beings; joy in revering and making offerings to your masters; joy in spreading the practice of charity (dāna); joy in firmly keeping the rules of discipline (śīla); joy in forbearance (kṣānti); joy in unflinching zeal (vīrya) to sow all excellent roots; joy in unperturbed serenity (dhyāna); joy in wiping out all defilement that screens clear wisdom (prajñā); joy in expanding the enlightened (bodhi) mind; joy in overcoming all demons; joy in eradicating all troubles (kleśa); joy in purifying the Buddha land; joy in winning merits from excellent physical marks; joy in embellishing the bodhimaṇḍala (the holy site); joy in fearlessness to hear (and understand) the profound Dharma; joy in the three perfect doors to nirvāṇa (i.e. voidness, formlessness and inactivity) as contrasted with their incomplete counterparts (which still cling to the notion of objective realization); joy of being with those studying the same Dharma and joy in the freedom from hindrance when amongst those who do not study it; joy to guide and convert evil men and to be with men of good counsel; joy in the state of purity and cleanness; joy in the practice of countless conditions contributory to enlightenment. All this is the Bodhisattva joy in the Dharma.'

"Thereat, the demon said to the girls: 'I want you all to return with me to our palace.'

"The girls replied: 'While we are here with the venerable upāsaka, we delight in the joy of the Dharma; we no longer want the five kinds of worldly pleasures.'

"The demon then said to Vimalakīrti: 'Will the upāsaka give away all these girls, as he who gives away everything to others is a Bodhisattva?'

"Vimalakīrti said: 'I now give up all of them and you can

take them away so that all living beings can fulfil their vows to realize the Dharma.'[1]

"The girls then asked Vimalakīrti: 'What should we do while staying at the demon's palace?'

"Vimalakīrti replied: 'Sisters, there is a Dharma called the *Inexhaustible Lamp* which you should study and practise. For instance, a lamp can (be used to) light up hundreds and thousands of other lamps; darkness will thus be bright and this brightness will be inexhaustible. So, sisters, a Bodhisattva should guide and convert hundreds and thousands of living beings so that they all develop the mind set on supreme enlightenment; thus his deep thought (of enlightening others) is, likewise, inexhaustible. His expounding of the Dharma will then increase in all excellent Dharmas; this is called the Inexhaustible Lamp. Although you will be staying at the demon's palace you should use this Inexhaustible Lamp to guide countless sons and daughters of devas to develop their minds set on supreme enlightenment, in order to repay your debt of gratitude to the Buddha, and also for the benefit of all living beings.'

"The devas' daughters bowed their heads at Vimalakīrti's feet and followed the demon to return to his palace; and all of a sudden they vanished. World Honoured One, since Vimalakīrti possesses such supernatural power, wisdom and eloquence, I am not qualified to call on him to enquire after his health."

The Buddha then said to a son of an elder called Excellent Virtue: "You call on Vimalakīrti to enquire after his health on my behalf."

[1] Vimalakīrti gave the girls back to the demon whose wish was thus granted, and took the opportunity to teach them to develop the supreme bodhi mind to fulfil his own vow to liberate all living beings. So both the demon's vow and that of Vimalakīrti were fulfilled, which is what a Bodhisattva should do in his work of salvation.

Excellent Virtue said: "World Honoured One, I am not qualified to call on him to enquire after his health. The reason is that once I held a ceremonial meeting at my father's house to make offerings to the gods and also to monks, brahmins, poor people, outcastes and beggars. When the meeting ended seven days later, Vimalakīrti came and said to me: 'O son of the elder, an offering meeting should not be held in the way you did; it should bestow the Dharma upon others, for what is the use of giving alms away?'

"I asked: 'Venerable Upāsaka, what do you mean by bestowal of Dharma?'

"He replied: 'The bestowal of Dharma is (beyond the element of time, having) neither start nor finish, and each offering should benefit all living beings at the same time. This a bestowal of Dharma.'

"I asked: 'What does this mean?'

"He replied: 'This means that bodhi springs from kindness (maitrī)[1] toward living beings; the salvation of living beings springs from compassion (karuṇā); the upholding of right Dharma from joy (muditā); wisdom from indifference (upekṣā);[2] the overcoming of greed from charity-perfection (dāna-pāramitā); ceasing to break the precepts from discipline-perfection (śīla-pāramitā); egolessness from patience-perfection (kṣānti-pāramitā); relinquishment of body and mind from zeal-perfection (vīrya-pāramitā);

[1] Because of one's boundless kindness to all living beings one seeks bodhi to save them.

[2] These are called the four immeasurables, or infinite states of minds: boundless kindness, maitrī, or giving of joy or happiness; boundless compassion, karuṇā, to save from suffering; boundless joy, muditā, on seeing others rescued from suffering; and limitless indifference, upekṣā, i.e. rising above these emotions, or giving up all things, such as distinction of friend and foe, like and dislike, etc. They are also called the four equalities or universals, and the four noble acts of pure living which ensure rebirth in the Brahmaloka or the heavens of form.

realization of enlightenment from serenity-perfection (dhyāna-pāramitā); realization of all-knowledge (sarvajña) from wisdom-perfection (prajñā-pāramitā); the teaching and converting of living beings spring from the void; non-rejection of worldly activities springs from formlessness; appearance in the world springs from inactivity;[1] sustaining the right Dharma from the power of expedient devices (upāya); the liberation of living beings from the four winning virtues;[2] respect for and service to others from the determination to wipe out arrogance; the relinquishment of body, life and wealth from the three indestructibles;[3] the six thoughts to dwell upon[4] from concentration on the Dharma; the six points of reverent harmony in a monastery[5] from the straightforward mind; right deeds from pure livelihood; joy in the pure mind from nearness to saints and sages; non-rising of hate for bad people from the effective control of mind; retiring from the world from the profound mind; practice in accordance with the preaching from the wide knowledge gained from hearing (about the Dharma); absence of disputation from a leisurely life; the quest of Buddha wisdom from meditation; the freeing of living beings from bondage from actual practice; the earning of all

[1] This refers to the three gates to the city of nirvāṇa which can be entered by meditation on *voidness* which empties the mind of the idea of the self and others; on *formlessness* which wipes out form or externals; and on *inactivity* which puts an end to all worldly activities while appearing in the world to deliver all living beings.

[2] The four Bodhisattva winning actions, see p. 10, n. 2.

[3] The three indestructibles: infinite body, endless life and boundless spiritual possessions.

[4] The six thoughts to dwell upon: Buddha, Dharma, Saṅgha, the commandments, almsgiving and heaven with its prospective happiness.

[5] The six points of reverent harmony or unity in a monastery: bodily unity in the form of worship; verbal unity in chanting; mental unity in faith; moral unity in observing the commandments; doctrinal unity in views and interpretations; and economic unity in community of goods, deeds, studies or charity.

excellent physical marks to embellish Buddha lands from the karma of moral excellence; the knowledge of the minds of all living beings and the relevant expounding of Dharma to them, from the karma of good knowledge; the understanding of all things commensurate with neither acceptance nor rejection of them to realize their oneness, from the karma of wisdom; the eradication of all troubles (kleśa), hindrances and evils from all excellent karmas; the realization of all wisdom and good virtues from the contributory conditions leading to enlightenment.[1] All this, son of good family, pertains to the bestowal of Dharma. A Bodhisattva holding this meeting that bestows the Dharma, is a great almsgiver (dānapati); he is also a field of blessedness for all worlds.'

"World Honoured One, as Vimalakīrti was expounding the Dharma, two hundred Brahmins who listened to it, set their minds on the quest of supreme enlightenment. I myself realized purity and cleanness of mind which I had never experienced before. I then bowed my head at his feet and took out my priceless necklace of precious stones which I offered to him but he refused it. I then said. 'Venerable Upāsaka, please accept my present and do what you like with it.' He took my necklace and divided it in two, offering half to the poorest beggar in the assembly and the other half to the 'Invincible Tathāgata' whose radiant land was then visible to all those present, who saw the half-necklace transformed into a precious tower in all its majesty on four pillars which did not shield one another. After this supernatural transformation, Vimalakīrti said: 'He who gives alms to the poorest beggar with an impartial mind performs an act which does not differ from the field of blessedness of the

[1] i.e. the thirty-seven contributory conditions to enlightenment. See p. 10, nn. 4-5 and p. 11, nn. 1-6.

Tathāgata, for it derives from great compassion with no expectation of reward. This is called the complete bestowal of Dharma.'

"After witnessing Vimalakīrti's supernatural power, the poorest beggar who had also listened to his expounding of the Dharma developed a mind set on supreme enlightenment. Hence I am not qualified to call on Vimalakīrti to enquire after his health."

Thus each of the Bodhisattvas present related his encounter with Vimalakīrti and declined to call on him to enquire after his health.

CHAPTER FIVE

Mañjuśrī's Call on Vimalakīrti

THE Buddha then said to Mañjuśrī: "You call on Vimalakīrti to enquire after his health."

Mañjuśrī said: "World Honoured One, he is a man of superior wisdom and it is not easy to match him (in eloquence). For he has reached reality, and is a skilful expounder of the essentials of the Dharma. His power of speech is unhindered and his wisdom is boundless. He is well versed in all matters pertaining to Bodhisattva development for he has entered the mysterious treasury of all Buddhas. He has overcome all demons, has achieved all transcendental powers[1] and has realized wisdom by ingenious devices (upāya). Nevertheless, I will obey the holy command and will call on him to enquire after his health."

The Bodhisattvas, the chief disciples of the Buddha and the rulers of the four heavens who were present, thought to themselves: "As the two Mahāsattvas will be meeting, they will certainly discuss the profound Dharma." So, eight thousand Bodhisattvas, five hundred śrāvakas and hundreds and thousands of devas wanted to follow Mañjuśrī.

So Mañjuśrī, reverently surrounded by the Bodhisattvas, the Buddha's chief disciples and the devas, made for Vaiśālī town. Vimalakīrti, who knew in advance that Mañjuśrī and his followers would come, used his transcendental powers to empty his house of all attendants and furniture except a sick bed.

[1] Lit. "in which the Buddhas and Bodhisattvas indulge, or take their pleasure".

When entering the house Mañjuśrī saw only Vimalakīrti lying on a sick bed, and was greeted by the upāsaka who said: "Welcome, Mañjuśrī, you come with no idea of coming and you see with no idea of seeing."[1]

Mañjuśrī replied: "It is so, Venerable Upāsaka, coming should not be further tied to (the idea of) coming, and going should not be further linked with (the concept of) going. Why? Because there is neither whence to come nor whither to go, and that which is visible cannot further be (an object of) seeing.[2] Now, let us put all this aside. Venerable Upāsaka, is your illness bearable? Will it get worse by wrong treatment? The World Honoured One sends me to enquire after your health, and is anxious to have good news of you. Venerable Upāsaka, where does your illness come from; how long has it arisen, and how will it come to an end?"

Vimalakīrti replied: "Stupidity leads to love which is the origin of my illness. Because all living beings are subject to illness I am ill as well. When all living beings are no longer ill, my illness will come to an end. Why? A Bodhisattva, because of (his vow to save) living beings, enters the realm of birth and death which is subject to illness; if they are all cured the Bodhisattva will no longer be ill. For instance, when the only son of an elder falls ill, so do his parents, and when he recovers his health, so do they. Likewise, a Bodhisattva loves all living beings as if they were his sons; so when they fall ill, the Bodhisattva is also ill, and when they recover, he is no longer ill."

Mañjuśrī asked: "What is the cause of a Bodhisattva's illness?"

[1] i.e. without being held in bondage by discrimination concerning coming and seeing.

[2] This is to avoid creating a duality of subject and object so as to preserve the absolute function of seeing.

Vimalakīrti replied: "A Bodhisattva's illness comes from (his) great compassion."

Mañjuśrī asked: "Why is the Venerable Upāsaka's house empty and without servants?"

Vimalakīrti replied: "All Buddha lands are also void."

Mañjuśrī asked: "Of what is the Buddha land void?"

Vimalakīrti replied: "It is void of voidness."[1]

Mañjuśrī asked: "Why should voidness be void?"[2]

Vimalakīrti replied: "Voidness is void in the absence of discrimination."

Mañjuśrī asked: "Can voidness be subject to discrimination?"

Vimalakīrti replied: "All discrimination is also void."

Mañjuśrī asked: "Where can voidness be sought?"

Vimalakīrti replied: "It should be sought in the sixty-two false views."[3]

Mañjuśrī asked: "Where should the sixty-two false views be sought?"

Vimalakīrti replied: "They should be sought in the liberation of all Buddhas."

Mañjuśrī asked: "Where should the liberation of all Buddhas be sought?"

Vimalakīrti replied: "It should be sought in the minds of all living beings." He continued: "The virtuous one has also asked why I have no servants; well, all demons and heretics are my servants. Why? Because demons like (the state of) birth and death which the Bodhisattva does not reject,

1 Mañjuśrī meant: "Your house is void because it is empty of objects and servants, but of what is the Buddha land void?" Vimalakīrti meant: "In the absolute state of Buddhahood, even wisdom should not be clung to in order to realize the voidness of both subject and object."

2 Mañjuśrī meant: "Since all things are fundamentally void in the absolute Buddha land, why should wisdom also be void to make them void once more?"

3 The sixty-two false views: see p. 33, n. 1 for detailed explanations.

whereas heretics delight in false views in the midst of which the Bodhisattva remains unmoved."

Mañjuśrī asked: "What form does the Venerable Upāsaka's illness take?"

Vimalakīrti replied: "My illness is formless and invisible."

Mañjuśrī asked: "Is it an illness of the body or of the mind?"

Vimalakīrti replied: "It is not an illness of the body for it is beyond body, and it is not that of the mind for the mind is like an illusion."

Mañjuśrī asked: "Of the four elements, earth, water, fire and air, which one is ill?"

Vimalakīrti replied: "It is not an illness of the element of earth but it is not beyond it; it is the same with the other elements of water, fire and air. Since the illnesses of all living beings originate from the four elements which cause them to suffer, I am ill too."

Mañjuśrī then asked: "What should a Bodhisattva say when comforting another Bodhisattva who falls ill?"

Vimalakīrti replied: "He should speak of the impermanence of the body but never of the abhorrence and relinquishment of the body. He should speak of the suffering body but never of the joy in nirvāṇa. He should speak of egolessness in the body while teaching and guiding all living beings (in spite of the fact that they are fundamentally non-existent in the absolute state). He should speak of the voidness of the body but should never cling to the ultimate nirvāṇa. He should speak of repentance of past sins but should avoid slipping into the past. Because of his own illness he should take pity on all those who are sick. Knowing that he has suffered during countless past aeons he should think of the welfare of all living beings. He should think of his past practice of good virtues to uphold (his determination for) right livelihood. Instead of worrying about troubles (kleśa) he should give rise to zeal and devotion (in his practice of the Dharma). He should act like a king physician to cure others' illnesses. Thus a Bodhisattva should comfort another sick Bodhisattva to make him happy."

Mañjuśrī asked: "How does a sick Bodhisattva control his mind?"

Vimalakīrti replied: "A sick Bodhisattva should think thus: 'My illness comes from inverted thoughts and troubles (kleśa) during my previous lives but it has no real nature of its own. (Therefore,) who is suffering from it? Why is it so? (Because) when the four elements unite to form a body, the former are ownerless and the latter is egoless. Moreover, my illness comes from my clinging to an ego; hence I should wipe out this clinging.'

"Now that he knows the source of his illness, he should forsake the concept of an ego and a living being. He should think of things (dharma) thus: 'A body is created by the union of all sorts of dharmas (elements) which alone rise and fall, without knowing one another and without announcing their rise and fall.' In order to wipe out the concept of things (dharmas) a sick Bodhisattva should think thus: 'This notion of dharma is also an inversion which is my great calamity. So I should keep from it.' What is to be kept from? From both subject and object. What does this keeping from subject and object mean? It means keeping from dualities. What does this keeping from dualities mean? It means not thinking of inner and outer dharmas (i.e. contraries) by the practice of impartiality. What is impartiality? It means equality (of all contraries e.g.) ego and nirvāṇa. Why is it so? Because both ego and nirvāṇa are void. Why are both void? Because they exist only by names which have no independent nature of their own.

"When you achieve this equality you are free from all illnesses but there remains the conception of voidness which also is an illusion and should be wiped out as well.

"A sick Bodhisattva should free himself from the conception of sensation (vedanā) when experiencing any one of its three states (which are painful, pleasurable and neither painful nor pleasurable feeling). Before his full development into Buddhahood (that is before delivering all living beings in his own mind) he should not wipe out vedanā for his own benefit with a view to attaining nirvāṇa for himself only. Knowing that the body is subject to suffering he should think of living beings in the lower realms of existence and give rise to compassion (for them). Since he has succeeded in controlling his false views, he should guide all living beings to bring theirs under control as well. He should uproot their (inherent) illnesses without (trying to) wipe out non-existent dharmas (externals or sense data). For he should teach them how to cut off the origin of illnesses. What is the origin of illnesses? It is their clinging which causes their illnesses. What are the objects of their clinging? They are the three realms (of desire, form and beyond form). By what means should they cut off their clinging? By means (of the doctrine that) nothing whatsoever can be found, and (that) if nothing can be found there will be no clinging. What is meant by 'nothing can be found'? It means (that) apart from dual views (there is nothing else that can be had). What are dual views? They are inner and outer views beyond which there is nothing.[1]

"Mañjuśrī, this is how a sick Bodhisattva should control his mind. To wipe out suffering from old age, illness and death is the Bodhisattva's bodhi (enlightened practice). If he fails to do so his practice lacks wisdom and is unprofitable.

[1] Inner discrimination and outer sense data; both are non-existent.

For instance, a Bodhisattva is (called) courageous if he overcomes hatred; if in addition he wipes out (the concept of) old age, illness and death he is a true Bodhisattva.

"A sick Bodhisattva should again reflect: Since my illness is neither real nor existing, the illnesses of all living beings are also unreal and non-existent. But while so thinking if he develops a great compassion derived from his love for living beings and from his attachment to this false view, he should (immediately) keep from these feelings. Why is it so? Because a Bodhisattva should wipe out all external causes of troubles (kleśa) while developing great compassion. For (this) love and (these) wrong views result from hate of birth and death. If he can keep from this love and these wrong views he will be free from hatred, and wherever he may be reborn he will not be hindered by love and wrong views. His next life will be free from obstructions and he will be able to expound the Dharma to all living beings and free them from bondage. As the Buddha has said, there is no such thing as untying others when one is still held in bondage for it is possible to untie others only after one is free from bonds.

"Therefore, a Bodhisattva should not tie himself up (with wrong views). What is tying and what is untying? Clinging to serenity (dhyāna) is a Bodhisattva's bondage, but his expedient rebirth (for the salvation of others) is freedom from bondage. Further, he is held in bondage by wisdom which lacks expedient methods (upāya), but is liberated by wisdom supported by expedient devices; he is (also) held in bondage by expedient methods which are not upheld by wisdom but is liberated by expedient methods backed by wisdom.

"What is bondage by wisdom unsupported by expedient methods? It is bondage caused by the Bodhisattva's desire to embellish the Buddha land (with merits) in order to bring living beings to perfection while practising for his self-control (the three gates to nirvāṇa, namely,) voidness, formlessness and inactivity. This is called bondage by wisdom unsupported by expedient methods (upāya).

"What is liberation by wisdom backed by expedient methods? It is liberation achieved in the absence of desire to embellish the Buddha land (with merits) in order to bring living beings to perfection, while practising unremittingly for his self-control (the three gates to nirvāṇa, namely) voidness, formlessness and inactivity. This is called liberation by wisdom supported by expedient methods (upāya).[1]

"What is bondage by expedient methods unsupported by wisdom? It is bondage caused by a Bodhisattva's lack of determination to keep from desire, anger, perverse views and other troubles (kleśa) while planting all wisdom roots. This is called bondage by expedient methods which lack wisdom.

"What is liberation by expedient methods sustained by wisdom? It is liberation won by a Bodhisattva who keeps

[1] In the Diamond Sūtra, the Buddha asks: "Subhūti, what do you think? Do Bodhisattvas adorn Buddha lands by their moral actions?" Subhūti replied: "No, World Honoured One. Why? Because this is not real adornment . . ." The Buddha said: "Subhūti, this is why all Bodhisattvas and Mahāsattvas should thus develop a pure and clean mind which should not abide in form, sound, taste, touch and dharma (things). They should develop a mind which does not abide anywhere." (See Ch'an and Zen Teaching, Series One, Part III, *The Diamond Cutter of Doubts*, p. 173. Rider, London; Shambala, Berkeley)

In the same sūtra, Subhūti asked: "Why do Bodhisattvas not receive reward for their merits?" The Buddha replied: "Bodhisattvas should have no longing and no attachment when they practise meritorious virtues; therefore, they do not receive a reward." (See Ch'an and Zen Teaching, Series One, p. 200. Rider, London; Shambala, Berkeley)

from desire, anger, perverse views and other troubles (kleśa) while planting all virtuous roots which he dedicates to his realization of supreme enlightenment. This is called liberation by expedient methods sustained by wisdom.

"Mañjuśrī, a sick Bodhisattva should look into all things in this way. He should further meditate on his body which is impermanent, is subject to suffering and is non-existent and egoless; this is called wisdom. Although his body is sick he remains in (the realm of) birth and death for the benefit of all (living beings) without complaint; this is called expedient method (upāya).

"He should further meditate on the body which is inseparable from illness and on illness which is inherent in the body because sickness and the body are neither new nor old; this is called wisdom. The body, though ill, is not to be annihilated; this is the expedient method (for remaining in the world to work for salvation).

"Mañjuśrī, a sick Bodhisattva should thus control his mind while dwelling in neither the (state of) controlled mind nor its opposite, that of uncontrolled mind. For if he dwells in (the state of) uncontrolled mind, this is stupidity and if he dwells in (that of) controlled mind, this is the śrāvaka stage. Hence a Bodhisattva should not dwell in either and so keep from both; this is the practice of the Bodhisattva stage. When staying in the realm of birth and death he keeps from its impurity, and when dwelling in nirvāṇa he keeps from (its condition of) extinction of reincarnation and escape from suffering; this is the practice of the Bodhisattva stage. That which is neither worldly nor saintly is Bodhisattva development (into Buddhahood). That which is neither impure nor pure is Bodhisattva practice. Although he is beyond the demonic state he appears (in the world) to overcome demons; this is Bodhisattva conduct. In his quest of all knowledge (sarvajña) he does not seek it at an inappropriate moment;[1] this is Bodhisattva conduct. Although he looks into the uncreate he does not achieve Buddhahood; this is Bodhisattva conduct. Although he looks into nidāna (or the twelve links in the chain of existence)[2] he enters all states of perverse views (to save living beings); this is Bodhisattva conduct. Although he helps all living beings he does not give rise to clinging; this is Bodhisattva conduct. Although he keeps from the phenomenal he does not lean on the voidness of body and mind; this is Bodhisattva conduct. Although he passes through the three worlds (of desire, form and beyond form) he does not injure the Dharmatā;[3] this is the Bodhisattva conduct. Although he realizes the voidness (of things) he sows the seeds of all merits; this is Bodhisattva conduct. Although he dwells in formlessness he continues delivering living beings; this is Bodhisattva conduct. Although he refrains from (creative) activities he appears in his physical body; this is Bodhisattva conduct. Although he keeps (all thoughts) from rising he performs all good deeds; this is Bodhisattva conduct. Although he practises the six perfections (pāramitās)[4] he knows all the mental states of living beings; this is Bodhisattva conduct. Although he possesses the six supernatural powers[5] he refrains from putting an end to all worldly streams;[6] this is Bodhisattva conduct. Although he practises the four infinite states of

[1] He should not seek the Buddha's all-knowledge before his full development into Buddhahood.

[2] The twelve links in the chain of existence, see p. 40, n. 4 for detailed explanation.

[3] Dharmatā, the underlying nature of all things.

[4] The six perfections or pāramitās, see p. 1, n. 1.

[5] The six supernatural powers, see p. 19, n. 1.

[6] So that he can stay in the world to continue his salvation work.

mind,[1] he does not wish to be reborn in the Brahma heavens;[2] this is Bodhisattva conduct. Although he practises meditation,[3] serenity (dhyāna),[4] liberation[5] and samādhi,[6] he does not avail himself of these to be reborn in dhyāna heavens;[7] this is Bodhisattva conduct. Although he practises the fourfold state of mindfulness[8] he does not keep for ever from the karma of body and mind;[9] this is Bodhisattva conduct.[10] Although he practises the four right efforts[11] he persists in physical and mental zeal and devotion; this is Bodhisattva conduct. Although he practises the four Hīnayāna steps to supernatural powers[12] he will continue doing so until he

[1] The four infinite states of mind, see p. 45, n. 2.

[2] Because the successful practice of the four infinite states of mind ensures a rebirth in the Brahma heavens which handicaps the Bodhisattva development into Buddhahood.

[3] This means the four states of meditation on the heaven of form: in the first heaven where the inhabitants are without the organs of taste or smell, not needing food, but possess the other four organs; in the second heaven where the inhabitants have ceased to require the five physical organs, possessing only that of mind; in the third where the inhabitants still have the organ of mind and are receptive of great joy; and in the fourth they still have mind which is very subtle.

[4] The four states of serenity in the formless heavens: in the first heavens where the mind becomes void and vast like space; in the second where the powers of perception and understanding are unlimited; in the third where the discriminative powers of mind are subdued; and in the fourth where intuitive wisdom appears.

[5] Liberation in eight forms or aṣṭa-vimokṣa, see p. 24, n. 1.

[6] Samādhi achieved through the three gates to the city of nirvāṇa: voidness, formlessness and inactivity.

[7] He thus sows causes without reaping their effects to show his sovereign independence from the law of causality in order to avoid a rebirth in the dhyāna heavens so that he can continue his Bodhisattva development into Buddhahood.

[8] The four states of mindfulness (smṛtyupasthāna), see p. 10, n. 5.

[9] The karma of body or evil karma of the five sense organs in the world of desire; and the karma of mind or good karma in the heavens of form.

[10] So that he can be in touch with all living beings in order to liberate them.

[11] The four right efforts (samyakprahāṇa), see p. 11, n. 1.

[12] The four Hīnayāna steps to supernatural powers (ṛddhipāda), see p. 11, n. 2.

achieves all Mahāyāna supernatural powers;[1] this is Bodhisattva conduct. Although he practises the five spiritual faculties[2] of the śrāvaka stage he discerns the sharp and dull potentialities of living beings; this is Bodhisattva conduct. Although he practises the five powers[3] of the śrāvaka stage he strives to achieve the ten powers of the Buddha;[4] this is Bodhisattva conduct. Although he practises the seven Hīnayāna degrees of enlightenment[5] he discerns the Buddha's all-wisdom (sarvajña); this is Bodhisattva conduct. Although he practises the eightfold noble truth (of Hinayāna)[6] he delights in treading the Buddha's boundless path; this is Bodhisattva conduct. Although he practises śamatha-vipaśyanā[7] which contributes to the realization of bodhi (enlightenment) he keeps from slipping into nirvāṇa; this is Bodhisattva conduct. Although he practises the doctrine of not creating and not annihilating things (dharma) he still embellishes his body with the excellent physical marks of the Buddha; this is Bodhisattva conduct. Although he appears as a śrāvaka or a pratyeka-buddha, he does not stray from the Buddha Dharma; this is Bodhisattva conduct. Although he has realized ultimate purity he appears in bodily form to do his work of salvation; this is Bodhisattva conduct. Although he sees into all Buddha lands which are permanently still like space, he causes them to appear in their purity and cleanness; this is Bodhisattva conduct. Although he has reached the Buddha stage which enables him to turn

[1] The six Mahāyāna supernatural powers, see p. 19, n. 1.

[2] The five spiritual faculties (pañca-indriyāṇi), see p. 1, n. 3.

[3] The five powers of the śrāvaka stage (pañca-balāni), see p. 11, n. 4.

[4] The Buddha's ten powers (daśabala), see p. 2, n. 1.

[5] The seven Hīnayāna degrees of enlightenment (sapta-bodhyaṅga), see p. 11, n. 5.

[6] The eightfold noble path (aṣṭa-mārga), see p. 11, n. 6.

[7] Śamatha-vipaśyanā or chih kuan in Chinese: see *The Secrets of Chinese Meditation*, p. 111. (Rider, London; Weiser, New York)

the wheel of the Law (to preach the Dharma) and to enter the state of nirvāṇa, he does not forsake the Bodhisattva path; this is Bodhisattva conduct."

While Vimalakīrti was expounding the Dharma, all the eight thousand sons of devas who had come with Mañjuśrī, developed the profound mind set on the quest of supreme enlightenment (anuttara-samyak-saṁbodhi).

CHAPTER SIX

The Inconceivable Liberation

ŚĀRIPUTRA saw no seats in the room and thought: "Where do the Bodhisattvas and chief disciples sit?" Vimalakīrti knew of Śāriputra's thought and asked him: "Virtuous One, do you come here for a seat or for the Dharma?" Śāriputra replied: "I come here for the Dharma and not for a seat."

Vimalakīrti said: "Hey Śāriputra, he who searches for the Dharma does not even cling to his body and life, still less to a seat, for the quest of Dharma is not related to (the five aggregates): form (rūpa), sensation (vedanā), conception (sañjñā), discrimination (saṁskāra) and consciousness (vijñāna); to the eighteen fields of sense (dhātu: the six organs, their objects and their perceptions); to the twelve entrances (āyatana: the six organs and six sense data that enter for or lead to discrimination); and to the worlds of desire, form and beyond form. Śāriputra, a seeker of the Dharma does not cling to the Buddha, the Dharma and the Saṅgha. A seeker of the Dharma does not hold the view of suffering, of cutting off all the accumulated causes thereof to put an end to it by treading the path to nirvāṇa (i.e. the four noble truths). Why is it so? Because the Dharma is beyond all sophistry. For if one says: 'Because I see suffering, I cut off its accumulated causes to wipe it out by treading the path thereto', this is mere sophistry and is not the quest of the Dharma.

"Śāriputra, the Dharma is called nirvāṇa (the condition of complete serenity and ultimate extinction of reincarnation);

if you give rise to (the concept of) birth and death, this is a search for birth and death and is not the quest of Dharma. The Dharma is (absolute and) immaculate, but if you are defiled by the (thought of) Dharma and even that of nirvāṇa, this is pollution which runs counter to the quest of Dharma. Dharma cannot be practised and if it is put into practice, this implies something (i.e. an object) to be practised and is not the quest of Dharma. Dharma is beyond grasping and rejecting, and if you grasp or reject it, this is grasping or rejecting (something else) but not the quest of Dharma. Dharma is beyond position but if you give it a place, this is clinging to space but not the quest of Dharma. Dharma is formless but if you rely on form to conceive the Dharma, this is search for form but not the quest of Dharma. Dharma is not an abode but if you want to stay in it this is dwelling in (an objective) Dharma, but not the quest of (absolute) Dharma. Dharma can be neither seen, nor heard nor felt nor known but if you want to see, hear, feel and know it, this is the functioning of your (discriminatory) seeing, hearing, feeling and knowing but not the quest of Dharma. Dharma is (transcendentally) inactive (wu wei) but if you are set on worldly activities, this is a search for the worldly way of life but not the quest of Dharma. Therefore, Śāriputra, the quest of Dharma does not imply seeking anything whatsoever."

When Vimalakīrti so spoke, five hundred sons of devas realized the pure Dharma Eye.[1]

Vimalakīrti then asked Mañjuśrī: "The Virtuous One has travelled in countless thousands and tens of thousands of lakhs[2] of worlds; which one is the Buddha land

[1] Dharma eye: see p. 33, n. 3.

[2] Lakh or lac: a hundred thousand or any large indefinite number.

where the highest merits make the lion throne (of its Buddha)?"[1]

Mañjuśrī replied: "Venerable Upāsaka, in the east there is a Buddha land which is separated from here by a distance represented by worlds as countless as the sand grains in thirty-six Ganges rivers; it is called Merudhvaja whose Buddha is called Merukalpa who is still there. His body is 84,000 yojana[2] high and his lion throne, also as high, is of prominent majesty."

Thereat, Vimalakīrti used his transcendental powers to invite Buddha Merukalpa to send to his room thirty-two thousand high, large, majestic and clean lion thrones which the Bodhisattvas, chief disciples of the Buddha (Śākyamuni), Indra and Brahmā, the four deva kings, etc., had never seen before. The room contained all the thirty-two thousand lion thrones which did not hinder one another and which did not obstruct anything at Vaiśālī, in Jambudvīpa (our earth) and in the four heavens where all things remained unchanged as before.

Vimalakīrti then said to Mañjuśrī: "Please take a lion throne and be seated amongst the great Bodhisattvas by enlarging the size of your body to that of the seat." Those Bodhisattvas who had acquired supernatural powers, enlarged their bodies to the size of the thrones on which they sat (without difficulty). But the newly initiated Bodhisattvas and chief disciples of the Buddha could not mount the high thrones.

[1] Kumārajīva, who translated this sūtra into Chinese, commented: "Although Vimalakīrti already knows that Buddha land, he purposely asks Mañjuśrī so as to cause those present to develop faith in those highest merits of its Buddha in order to encourage them to perform the Bodhisattva deeds leading to those merits and also to convert the assembly by his fascinating acts of going to and returning from that Buddha land.

[2] Yojana: a distance covered by a royal day's march for the army in ancient India.

Vimalakīrti then said to Śāriputra: "Please be seated on a lion throne." Śāriputra replied: "Venerable Upāsaka, these thrones are large and high; we cannot mount them." Vimalakīrti said: "Śāriputra, you should first pay reverence to the Tathāgata Merukalpa and will then be able to sit on one of them."

Thereat, all newly initiated Bodhisattvas and chief disciples of the Buddha paid reverence to the Tathāgata Merukalpa and then sat on the lion thrones.

Śāriputra said to Vimalakīrti: "Venerable Upāsaka, this was not seen before; this small room can contain these high and large thrones which do not obstruct anything at Vaiśālī and do not interfere with the cities, towns and villages on Jambudvīpa (our world) as well as with the palaces of the devas and heavenly nāgas (dragons) and the abodes of the ghosts and spirits."

Vimalakīrti said: "Śāriputra, the liberation realized by all Buddhas and (great) Bodhisattvas is inconceivable. If a Bodhisattva wins this liberation he can put the great and extensive (Mount) Sumeru in a mustard seed which neither increases nor decreases (its size) while Sumeru remains the same, and the four deva kings (guardians of the world) and the devas of Trayastriṁśās (the heavens of Indra) are not even aware of their being put into the seed, but only those who have won liberation see Sumeru in the mustard seed. This is the inconceivable Dharma door to liberation.[1]

"He can also put the four great oceans (that surround

[1] There is nothing strange or extraordinary in this for a Buddha or Mahāsattva has succeeded in looking into the great and extensive Sumeru and the tiny mustard seed which are both phenomena having no nature of their own and are, therefore, void and non-existent. And a void and non-existent thing added to another void and non-existent thing will produce nothing nor will they hinder each other. In this and the following instances, space is wiped out.

Sumeru) in a pore without causing inconvenience to fishes, water tortoises, sea-turtles, water-lizards and all other aquatic animals while the oceans remain the same and the nāgas (dragons), ghosts, spirits and asuras (titans) are not even aware of being displaced and interposed.

"Further, Śāriputra, a great Bodhisattva who has won this inconceivable liberation can (take and) put on his right palm the great chiliocosm[1] like a potter holding his wheel, throw it beyond a number of worlds as countless as the sand grains in the Ganges, and then take it back (to its original place) while all living beings therein do not know of their being thrown away and returned and while our world remains unchanged.

"Further, Śāriputra, if there are living beings who are qualified for liberation but who want to stay longer in the world, this Bodhisattva will (use his supernatural power to) extend a week to an aeon so that they will consider (their remaining time) to be an aeon; and if on the other hand, there are living beings who hate staying longer in the world before achieving their liberation, this Bodhisattva will shorten an aeon to a week so that they will consider (their remaining time) to be one week.[2]

"Further, Śāriputra, a Bodhisattva who has won this inconceivable liberation can gather in one country all the majestic things of all Buddha lands so that they are all visible in that particular country.

"Further, he can place on his right palm all the living

[1] A great chiliocosm or tri-sahasra-mahā-sahasra-loka-dhātu: Mount Sumeru and its seven surrounding continents, eight seas and ring of mountains form one small world; 1,000 of these form a small chiliocosm; 1,000 of these small chiliocosms form a medium chiliocosm; 1,000 of these form a great chiliocosm, which consists of 1,000,000,000 small worlds.

[2] After wiping out space, the Bodhisattva in this instance, eliminates time as well.

beings of a Buddha land and then fly in all the ten directions to show them all things everywhere without even shaking them.

"Further, Śāriputra, this Bodhisattva can show through one of his pores all offerings to the Buddhas by living beings in the ten directions.

"He can show through one of his pores all suns, moons, planets and stars in all the worlds in the ten directions.

"Further, Śāriputra, he can breathe in (and hold in his mouth) all the winds blowing in the worlds in the ten directions without injuring his own body or the trees of these worlds.

"Further, when the worlds in the ten directions come to an end through destruction by fires, this Bodhisattva can breathe in these fires into his own belly without being injured by them while they continue to burn without change.

"Further, this Bodhisattva can take from the nadir a Buddha land separated from him by worlds as countless as the sand grains in the Ganges and lift it up to the zenith which is separated from him by worlds as countless as there are sand grains in the Ganges, with the same ease as he picks up a leaf of the date tree with the point of a needle.

"Further, Śāriputra, a Bodhisattva who has won this inconceivable liberation can use his transcendental powers to appear as a Buddha, or a pratyeka-buddha, a śrāvaka, a sovereign Śakra, Brahmā, or a ruler of the world (cakravartī). He can also cause all sound and voices of high, medium and low pitches in the worlds in the ten directions to change into the Buddha's voice proclaiming (the doctrine of) impermanence, suffering, unreality and absence of ego as well as all Dharmas expounded by all Buddhas in the ten directions, making them heard everywhere.

"Śāriputra, I have mentioned only some of the powers derived from this inconceivable liberation but if I were to enumerate them all, a whole aeon would be too short for the purpose."

Mahākāśyapa who had heard of this Dharma of inconceivable liberation, praised it and said it had never been expounded before. He then said to Śāriputra: "Like the blind who do not see images in various colours shown to them, all śrāvakas hearing this Dharma door to inconceivable liberation will not understand it. Of the wise men hearing about it, who will not set his mind on the quest of supreme enlightenment? What should we do to uproot for ever the rotten śrāvaka root as compared with this Mahāyāna, so that all śrāvakas hearing this doctrine of inconceivable liberation, shed tears of repentance and scream so loudly as to shake the great chiliocosm? As to the Bodhisattvas, they are all happy to receive this Dharma reverently by placing it on the tops of their heads. If a Bodhisattva believes and practises this Dharma door to inconceivable liberation, all demons cannot oppose him."

When Mahākāśyapa spoke these words, thirty-two thousand sons of the devas set their minds on the quest of supreme enlightenment.

Thereat, Vimalakīrti declared to Mahākāśyapa: "Virtuous One, those who appear as kings of demons in countless worlds in the ten directions are mostly Bodhisattvas who have realized this inconceivable liberation and who use expedient devices (upāya) to appear as their rulers in order to convert living beings.

"Further, Mahākāśyapa, countless Bodhisattvas in the ten directions appear as beggars asking for hands, feet, ears, noses, heads, brains, blood, flesh, skin and bones, towns and hamlets, wives and (female) slaves, elephants, horses, carts, gold, silver, lapis lazuli, agate, cornelian, coral, amber, pearl, jade shell, clothing, food and drink; most of these beggars are Bodhisattvas who have realized this inconceivable liberation and use expedient devices to test believers in order to cement their faith (in the Dharma). Because the Bodhisattvas who have realized inconceivable liberation possess the awe-inspiring power to bring pressure to bear upon (believers) and ask for inalienable things (to test them), but worldly men whose spirituality is low have no such (transcendental) powers and cannot do all this. These Bodhisattvas are like dragons and elephants which can trample (with tremendous force) which donkeys cannot do. This is called the wisdom and expedient methods (upāya) of the Bodhisattvas who have won inconceivable liberation."

CHAPTER SEVEN

Looking at Living Beings

MAÑJUŚRĪ asked Vimalakīrti: "How should a Bodhisattva look at living beings?"

Vimalakīrti replied: "A Bodhisattva should look at living beings like an illusionist does at the illusory men (he has created); and like a wise man looking at the moon's reflection in water; at his own face in a mirror; at the flame of a burning fire; at the echo of a calling voice; at flying clouds in the sky; at foam in a liquid; at bubbles on water; at the (empty) core of a banana tree; at a flash of lightning; at the (non-existent) fifth element (beside the four that make the human body); at the sixth aggregate (beside the five that make a sentient being); at the seventh sense datum (beside the six objects of sense); at the thirteenth entrance (āyatana—beside the twelve involving the six organs and six sense data); at the nineteenth realm of sense (beside the eighteen dhātus or fields of sense); at form in the formless world; at the (non-existent) sprout of a charred grain of rice; at a body seen by a śrota-āpanna (who has wiped out the illusory body to enter the holy stream); at the entry of an anāgāmin (or a non-returning śrāvaka) into the womb of a woman (for rebirth); at an arhat still preserving the three poisons (of desire, anger and stupidity which he has eliminated for ever); at a Bodhisattva realizing the patient endurance of the uncreate who is still greedy, resentful and breaking the prohibitions; at a Buddha still suffering from kleśa (troubles); at a blind man seeing things; at an adept who still breathes air in and out while in the state of nirvāṇic imperturbability; at the tracks of birds flying in the air; at the progeny of a barren woman; at the suffering of an illusory man; at a sleeping man seeing he is awake in a dream; at a devout man realizing nirvāṇa who takes a bodily form for (another) reincarnation; and at a smokeless fire.

"This is how a Bodhisattva should look at living beings."

Thereat, Mañjuśrī asked Vimalakīrti: "When a Bodhisattva so meditates how should he practise kindness (maitrī)?[1]

Vimalakīrti replied: "When a Bodhisattva has made this meditation, he should think that he ought to teach living beings to meditate in the same manner; this is true kindness. He should practise causeless (nirvāṇic) kindness which prevents creativeness; unheated kindness which puts an end to kleśa (troubles and causes of trouble); impartial kindness which covers all the three periods of time (which means that it is eternal involving past, future and present); passionless kindness which wipes out disputation; non-dual kindness which is beyond sense organs within and sense data without; indestructible kindness which eradicates all corruptibility;[2] stable kindness which is a characteristic of the undying self-mind; pure and clean kindness which is spotless like Dharmatā;[3] boundless kindness which is all-pervasive like space; the kindness of the arhat stage which destroys all bondage; the Bodhisattva kindness which gives comfort to living beings; the Tathāgata kindness which leads to the state of thatness; the Buddha kindness which enlightens all living beings; spontaneous kindness which is causeless; bodhi kindness which is of one flavour (i.e. uniform and unmixed wisdom); unsurpassed kindness which cuts off all

[1] Kindness (maitrī): see p. 45, n. 2.

[2] Indestructible kindness is a characteristic of the self-nature which is incorruptible.

[3] Dharmatā: see p. 58, n. 3.

desires; merciful kindness which leads to the Mahāyāna (path); untiring kindness because of deep insight into the void and non-existent ego; Dharma-bestowing (dāna) kindness which is free from regret and repentance; precepts (śīla) upholding kindness to convert those who have broken the commandments; patient (kṣānti) kindness which protects both the self and others; zealous (vīrya) kindness to liberate all living beings; serene (dhyāna) kindness which is unaffected by the five senses; wise (prajñā) kindness which is always timely; expedient (upāya) kindness to appear at all times for converting living beings; unhidden kindness because of the purity and cleanness of the straightforward mind; profound minded kindness which is free from discrimination; undeceptive kindness which is faultless; and joyful kindness which bestows the Buddha joy (in nirvāṇa).

"Such are the specialities of Bodhisattva kindness."

Mañjuśrī asked Vimalakīrti: "What should be his compassion (karuṇā)?"

Vimalakīrti replied: "His compassion should include sharing with all living beings all the merits he has won."

Mañjuśrī asked: "What should be his joy (muditā)?"

Vimalakīrti replied: "He should be filled with joy on seeing others win the benefit of the Dharma with no regret whatsoever."

Mañjuśrī asked "What should he relinquish (upekṣā)?"

Vimalakīrti replied: "In his work of salvation he should expect nothing (i.e. no gratitude or reward) in return."

Mañjuśrī asked: "On what should he rely in his fear of birth and death?"

Vimalakīrti replied: "He should rely on the power of the Tathāgata's moral merits."

Mañjuśrī asked: "What should he do to win support from the power of the Tathāgata's moral merits?"

Vimalakīrti replied: "He should liberate all living beings in order to win support from the power of the Tathāgata's moral merits."

Mañjuśrī asked: "What should he wipe out in order to liberate living beings?"

Vimalakīrti replied: "When liberating living beings he should wipe out their kleśa (troubles and causes of troubles)."

Mañjuśrī asked: "What should he do to wipe out kleśa?"

Vimalakīrti replied: "He should uphold right mindfulness."[1]

Mañjuśrī asked: "What should he do to uphold right mindfulness?"

Vimalakīrti replied: "He should advocate the unborn and the undying."

Mañjuśrī asked: "What is the unborn and what is the undying?"

Vimalakīrti replied: "The unborn is evil that does not arise and the undying is good that does not end."

Mañjuśrī asked: "What is the root of good and evil?"

Vimalakīrti replied: "The body is the root of good and evil."

Mañjuśrī asked: "What is the root of the body?"

Vimalakīrti replied: "Craving is the root of the body."

Mañjuśrī asked: "What is the root of craving?"

Vimalakīrti replied: "Baseless discrimination is the root of craving."

Mañjuśrī asked: "What is the root of baseless discrimination?"

Vimalakīrti replied: "Inverted thinking is the root of discrimination."

[1] Right mindfulness (samyaksmṛti) retains the true and keeps from the false.

Mañjuśrī asked: "What is the root of inverted thinking?"

Vimalakīrti replied: "Non-abiding is the root of inverted thinking."

Mañjuśrī asked: "What is the root of non-abiding?"

Vimalakīrti replied: "Non-abiding is rootless. Mañjuśrī, from this non-abiding root all things arise."

A goddess (devakanyā) who had watched the gods (devas) listening to the Dharma in Vimalakīrti's room appeared in bodily form to shower flowers on the Bodhisattvas and the chief disciples of the Buddha (in their honour). When the flowers fell on the Bodhisattvas, they fell to the ground, but when they fell on the chief disciples, they stuck to their bodies and did not drop in spite of all their efforts to shake them off.

Thereat, the goddess asked Śāriputra why he strove to shake the flowers off. Śāriputra replied: "I want to shake off these flowers which are not in the state of suchness." The goddess said: "Do not say these flowers are not in the state of suchness. Why? Because they do not differentiate, and it is you (alone) who give rise to differentiation. If you (still) differentiate after leaving home in your quest of Dharma, this is not the state of suchness, but if you no longer give rise to differentiation, this will be the state of suchness. Look at the Bodhisattvas whose bodies do not retain the flowers; this is because they have put an end to differentiation. This is like a man taking fright who invites trouble for himself from evil (people). So if a disciple fears birth and death, then form, sound, smell, taste and touch can trouble him, but if he is fearless he is immune from all the five sense data. (In your case) it is because the force of habit still remains that these flowers cleave to your body but if you cut it off, they will not stick to it."

Śāriputra asked: "How long have you been in this room?" The goddess replied: "My stay in this room is just like the

Venerable Elder's liberation."[1] Śāriputra asked: "Do you then mean that you have stayed here for a long time?" The goddess retorted: "Does your liberation also involve time?"[2] Śāriputra kept silent and did not reply. The goddess then asked: "Why is the wise elder silent on this point?" Śāriputra replied: "He who wins liberation does not express it in words; hence I do not know what to say."[3] The goddess said: "Spoken and written words reveal liberation. Why? For liberation is neither within nor without nor in between, and words also are neither inside nor outside nor in between. Therefore, Śāriputra, liberation cannot be preached without using words. Why? Because all things point to liberation."[4]

[1] Śāriputra was surprised by the goddess's eloquence and thought she must have been there for some time to listen to Vimalakīrti's teaching, thus implying the element of time in his question. The goddess taught him to wipe out the element of time in his quest of Mahāyāna and said that her stay in the absolute state was just what his own liberation should be, that is, beyond time and space.

[2] Śāriputra misunderstood the goddess's teaching and asked if she had stayed there for a considerable time, like his own liberation in the śrāvaka stage he had realized long ago. So the goddess retorted by asking if his own liberation implied time which is bondage instead of liberation. Thus the goddess wiped out the element of time.

[3] Śāriputra was called "Śāriputra, the Wise" because he had won great wisdom which distinguished him from the other chief disciples of the Buddha in the śrāvaka stage. (See *The Śūraṅgama Sūtra*, p. 1. Rider, London.)

[4] Time was wiped out in the preceding lines; here space is wiped out as well to expose the absolute.

The three dogmas of the middle or Mādhyamika school are: the immaterial noumenon, the material phenomenon, and the "mean" or the unifier which places each in the other and all in all. The doctrine opposes the rigid categories of existence (the material) and non-existence (the immaterial) and denies the two extremes in the interests of a middle or supreme way which is absolute being above and beyond all dualities, relativities and contraries.

Śāriputra spoke of the immaterial noumenon according to which liberation is beyond spoken and written words; hence his speechlessness. The goddess preached the "mean" according to which neither liberation nor words can be found within, without and in-between. Nevertheless, "liberation" is also a word which cannot be dropped when we speak of liberation. She meant that the immaterial cannot be revealed without using the material for both are neither unity nor diversity, pointing to the "mean" which is true liberation.

Śāriputra asked: "Do you then mean that there is no need to keep from carnality, hatred and stupidity to win liberation?"

The goddess replied: "In the presence of those who are proud (of their superior knowledge) the Buddha said it is important to keep from carnality, hatred and stupidity in the quest of liberation; but where they are absent, He said that the underlying nature of carnality, hatred and stupidity (i.e. the self-nature) is identical with liberation.[1]

Śāriputra exclaimed: "Excellent, goddess, excellent, what have you gained and experienced that gives you such an eloquence?"

The goddess replied: "The fact that I neither gain nor experience anything gives me this eloquence. Why is it so? Because he who (claims to) have won and experienced (something) is arrogant in the eye of the Buddha Dharma."

Śāriputra asked: "Which of the three vehicles[2] is your aim?"

The goddess replied: "When I preach the śrāvaka Dharma to convert people, I appear as a śrāvaka; when I expound the (twelve) links in the chain of existence I appear as a pratyeka-buddha; and when I teach great compassion to convert them, I appear as a (teacher of) Mahāyāna. Śāriputra, like those entering a campa[3] grove who smell only the fragrance of campas to the exclusion of all other odours, those entering this room smell only the fragrance of Buddha merits and no longer like the aroma of achievements by śrāvakas and pratyeka-buddhas.

[1] According to the Lotus Sūtra, there were some five thousand disciples who wrongly thought they had realized liberation and so refused to listen to this important sermon. But where there were no such arrogant people, the Buddha revealed that the underlying nature of sins is but liberation.

[2] The three vehicles (triyāna) by which śrāvakas, pratyeka-buddhas and Bodhisattvas attain their goals.

[3] Campa: a yellow fragrant flower in India.

"Śāriputra, when Indra, Brahmā, the four deva kings of the four heavens (guardians of the world), heavenly dragons, ghosts and spirits, etc. entered the room and heard this upāsaka (Vimalakīrti) expound the right Dharma, they all took delight in smelling the fragrance of Buddha merits and developed the Mahāyāna mind before returning to their worlds.

"Śāriputra, I have stayed here for twelve years during which I have never heard the Dharmas of śrāvakas and pratyeka-buddhas but only the doctrine of great kindness (maitrī) and great compassion (karuṇā) of the Bodhisattvas and the inconceivable Buddha Dharma.

"Śāriputra, in this room there are always eight unusual manifestations:

"Firstly, this room is illuminated by a golden light which is the same by day and by night and does not depend on either sunlight or moonlight to light it up;

"Secondly, he who enters it is immune from all troubles caused by defilements;

"Thirdly, this room is visited by Indra, Brahmā, the four deva kings of the four heavens and Bodhisattvas from other realms;

"Fourthly, the never-receding Dharma of the six pāramitās is always expounded in it;

"Fifthly, the most melodious heavenly music intoning countless Dharma doors (to enlightenment) is heard in it;

"Sixthly, this room contains the four canons (of sūtras, vinaya, śāstras and miscellaneous scriptures) full of inexhaustible precious treasures for those who are (spiritually) poor;

"Seventhly, when the venerable upāsaka thinks of Śākyamuni Buddha, Amitābha Buddha, Akṣobhya Buddha, the Buddha of Precious Virtues, the Buddha of Precious Flame, the Buddha of Precious Moonshine, the Buddha of Precious Majesty, the Invincible Buddha, the Buddha of the Lion's Roar, the Buddha of All-Perfection, and countless other Buddhas in the ten directions, they all come to expound the secrets of the esoteric Buddha Dharma, after which they return to their realms;

"Eighthly, all majestic heavenly palaces and all pure lands of Buddhas appear in this room.

"Śāriputra, after witnessing these eight remarkable things in this room, who still seeks the śrāvaka Dharma?"

Śāriputra asked: "Why do not you change your female bodily form?"

The goddess replied: "For the last twelve years I have been looking in vain for a female bodily form; so what do you want me to change? This is like an illusionist who creates an illusory woman; is it correct to ask him to change this unreal woman?"

Śāriputra said: "No, because it is not a real body; into what then can it be changed?"

The goddess said: "All phenomena (including forms) are also unreal. So why have you asked me to change my unreal female body?"

Thereat, she used her supernatural powers to change Śāriputra into a heavenly goddess and herself into a man similar to Śāriputra, and asked him: "Why do not you change your female form?"

Śāriputra replied: "I do not know why I have turned into a goddess."

The goddess said: "Śāriputra, if you can change your female body, all women should also be able to turn into men. Like Śāriputra who is not a woman but appears in female bodily form, all women are the same and though they appear in female form, they are fundamentally not women.

Hence the Buddha said: 'All things are neither male nor female'."

Thereat, the goddess again used her supernatural powers to change Śāriputra back to his (original) male body, and asked: "Where is your female body now?"

Śāriputra replied: "The form of a woman neither exists nor is non-existent."

The goddess then declared: "Likewise, all things are fundamentally neither existing nor non-existent, and that which neither exists nor is non-existent is proclaimed by the Buddha."[1]

Śāriputra asked: "When will you leave (die) here and where will you be reborn?"

The goddess replied: "I shall be reborn like a Buddha by transformation."

Śāriputra interjected: "The Buddha's transformation body implies neither birth nor death."

The goddess said: "Likewise all living beings (fundamentally) are subject to neither death nor birth."[2]

Śāriputra asked: "When will you realize supreme enlightenment (anuttara-samyak-saṁbodhi)?"

The goddess replied: "I shall realize supreme enlightenment when Śāriputra returns to the worldly way of life."[3]

Śāriputra retorted: "There is no such thing as myself (a holy man at the śrāvaka stage) returning to the worldly way of life."

The goddess said: "There is also no such thing as myself

[1] Reality or the absolute as proclaimed by the Buddha, is neither existing nor non-existent because it is absolute and is beyond all dualities, relativities and contraries.

[2] This reveals the changeless underlying nature of all living beings.

[3] To reveal that fundamentally there is no difference between the holy and the worldly, i.e. to cut short all discriminating.

realizing enlightenment. Why? Because bodhi (or enlightenment) is not an objective which can be realized."[1]

Śāriputra retorted: "There are Buddhas as countless as sand grains in the Ganges who have realized and will win supreme enlightenment; what will you say of them?"

The goddess said: "The three periods of time (the past, future and present) are spoken of (to the common man) as being in line with worldly thinking but this does not mean that bodhi (which is timeless or eternal) is tied to the past, future and present." She then asked Śāriputra: "Śāriputra, have you realized arhatship?"

Śāriputra replied: "I have realized it because I hold no concept of winning anything."

The goddess said: "Likewise, all Buddhas and great Bodhisattvas achieved their goals because they were free from the idea of winning supreme enlightenment."

Thereat, Vimalakīrti said to Śāriputra: "This goddess has made offerings to ninety-two lacs of Buddhas. She is able to play with the Bodhisattva transcendental powers, has fulfilled all her vows, has realized the patient endurance of the uncreate and has reached the never-receding Bodhisattva stage. In fulfilment of a vow, she appears at will (everywhere) to teach and convert living beings."

[1] To wipe out the dualism of subject and object.

CHAPTER EIGHT

The Buddha Path

MAÑJUŚRĪ asked Vimalakīrti: "How does a Bodhisattva enter the Buddha path?"

Vimalakīrti replied: "If a Bodhisattva treads the wrong ways (without discrimination) he enters the Buddha path."

Mañjuśrī asked: "What do you mean by a Bodhisattva treading the wrong ways?"

Vimalakīrti replied: "(In his work of salvation) if a Bodhisattva is free from irritation and anger while appearing in the fivefold uninterrupted hell;[1] is free from the stain of sins while appearing in (other) hells; is free from ignorance, arrogance and pride while appearing in the world of animals; is adorned with full merits while appearing in the world of hungry ghosts; does not show his superiority[2] while appearing in the (heavenly) worlds of form and beyond form; is immune from defilements while appearing in the world of desire; is free from anger while appearing as if he were resentful; uses wisdom to control his mind while appearing to be stupid; appears as if he were greedy but gives away all his outer (i.e. money and worldly) and inner (i.e. bodily) possessions without the least regret for his own life; appears as if he broke the prohibitions while delighting

[1] i.e. the avīci hell which is ceaseless in five respects (karma and its effects are an endless chain with no escape; it is timeless; its life is uninterrupted; its sufferings are endless; and it is ceaselessly full) resulting from the five deadly sins (parricide, matricide, killing an arhat; shedding the blood of a Buddha, and destroying the harmony of the saṅgha).

[2] Superiority felt by the gods over the five worlds under them.

in pure living and being apprehensive of committing even a minor fault; appears as if he were filled with hatred while always abiding in compassionate patience; appears as if he were remiss while diligently practising all meritorious virtues; appears as if he were disturbed while always remaining in the state of serenity; appears as if he were ignorant while possessing both mundane and supramundane wisdoms; appears as if he delighted in flattering and falsehood while he excells in expedient methods in conformity with straightforwardness as taught in the sūtras; shows arrogance and pride while he is as humble as a bridge;[1] appears as if he were tormented by troubles while his mind remains pure and clean; appears in the realm of demons while defeating heterodox doctrines to conform with the Buddha wisdom; appears in the realm of śrāvakas where he expounds the unheard of supreme Dharma; appears in the realm of pratyeka-buddhas where he converts living beings in fulfilment of great compassion; appears amongst the poor but extends to them his precious hands whose merits are inexhaustible;[2] appears amongst the crippled and disabled with his own body adorned with the excellent physical marks (of the Buddha); appears amongst the lower classes but grows the seed of the Buddha nature with all relevant merits; appears amongst the emaciated and ugly showing his strong body to the admiration of them all; appears as an old and ill man but is actually free from all ailments with no fear of death; appears as having all the necessities of life but always sees into impermanence and is free from greed;

[1] A Buddhist term which means that a Bodhisattva is like a bridge which is trampled upon without murmuring while serving all passers-by without distinction.

[2] i.e. the hand that bestows alms and precious things including the Buddha Dharma.

appears to have wives, concubines and maids but always keeps away from the morass of the five desires;[1] appears amongst the dull-witted and stammerers to help them win the power of speech derived from the perfect control of mind; appears amongst heretics to teach orthodoxy and deliver all living beings; enters all worlds of existence to help them uproot the causes leading thereto; and appears as if entering nirvāṇa but without cutting off birth and death;[2] Mañjuśrī, this Bodhisattva can tread heterodox ways because he has access to the Buddha path."[3]

Vimalakīrti then asked Mañjuśrī: "What are the seeds of the Tathāgata?"

Mañjuśrī replied: "Body is (a) seed of the Tathāgata; ignorance and craving are its (two) seeds; desire, hate and stupidity its (three) seeds; the four inverted views[4] its (four) seeds; the five covers (or screens)[5] its (five) seeds; the six organs of sense its (six) seeds; the seven abodes of consciousness[6] its (seven) seeds; the eight heterodox views[7] its (eight)

[1] The five desires arising from the objects of the five senses, things seen, heard, smelt, tasted and touched.

[2] So that he can stay in the world to deliver living beings.

[3] He already has access to the Buddha path and can, therefore, control his mind when entering these wrong ways.

[4] The four inverted views of existence, pleasure, ego and clearness in saṁsāra, in contrast with the transcendental reality of eternity, bliss, entity and purity in nirvāṇa as taught in the Mahāparinirvāṇa Sūtra.

[5] The five covers, screens or moral hindrances: desire, anger, drowsiness, agitation with regret, and doubt.

[6] The seven abodes of consciousness: 1, the first dhyāna heaven of Brahmā when he was alone at the beginning of an aeon; 2, this first dhyāna heaven with his later creation there of his people, where bodies differ but thinking is the same; 3, the second dhyāna heaven where bodies are identical but thinking differs; 4, the third dhyāna heaven where bodies and thinking are the same—the above dhyāna heavens are the worlds of form; 5, 6, and 7, are the first three formless heavens as explained by Kumārajīva, who translated this sūtra into Chinese.

[7] The opposites of the eightfold noble path.

seeds; the nine causes of kleśa (troubles and their causes)[1] its (nine) seeds; and the ten evils[2] its (ten) seeds. To sum up, all the sixty-two heterodox views[3] and all sorts of kleśa are the seeds of Buddhahood.[4]

Vimalakīrti asked Mañjuśrī: "Why is it so?"

Mañjuśrī replied: "Because he who perceives the inactive (wu wei) state and enters its right (nirvāṇic) position, is incapable of advancing further to achieve supreme enlightenment (anuttara-samyak-saṁbodhi).[5] For instance, high ground does not produce the lotus which grows only in marshy land. Likewise, those perceiving nirvāṇa and entering its right position, will not develop into Buddhahood, whereas living beings in the mire of kleśa can eventually develop the Buddha Dharma. This is also like seeds scattered in the void which do not grow, but if they are planted in manured fields they will yield good harvests. Thus, those entering the right position (of nirvāṇa) do not develop the Buddha Dharma, whereas those whose view of the ego is as great as (Mount) Sumeru may (because of the misery of life) eventually set their minds on the quest of

[1] Misplaced love of real enemies, unjustified hate of real friends and irritation caused by one's own body are the three causes which, multiplied by the three periods of time, past, future and present, total nine causes of troubles, as explained by Kumārajīva.

[2] The ten evils are: killing, stealing, carnality, lying, double tongue, coarse language, affected speech, covetousness, anger and wrong views.

[3] The sixty-two heterodox views: see p. 33, n. 1 for detailed explanations.

[4] If the above seeds of the Tathāgata are looked into they reveal the underlying nature of all things which is the absolute thatness. Hence the Ch'an school teaches its followers to be *clear* about their minds in order to *perceive* their underlying nature thereby *achieving* enlightenment or Buddhahood.

[5] Because relative nirvāṇa is attractive but lacks sufferings which are incentives to further progress on the Buddha path. Moreover, this attachment to nirvāṇa is also an hindrance to supreme enlightenment. This refers to śrāvakas and pratyeka-buddhas who are satisfied with their incomplete enlightenment and refuse to advance further.

supreme enlightenment, thereby developing the Buddha Dharma.

"Therefore, we should know that all sorts of kleśa are the seeds of the Tathāgata. This is like one who does not plunge into the ocean and will never find the priceless pearl. Likewise, a man who does not enter the ocean of kleśa will never win the gem of all-knowledge (sarvajña)."

Thereat, Mahākāśyapa exclaimed: "Excellent, Mañjuśrī, excellent, your sayings are most gratifying. As you have said, those suffering from kleśa are the seeds of the Tathāgata. So we are no longer capable of developing a mind set on enlightenment. Even those committing the five deadly sins[1] can eventually set their minds on the quest of the Buddha Dharma but we are unable to do so, like persons whose defective organs prevent them from enjoying the five objects of the senses. Likewise, the śrāvakas who have cut off all bonds (of transmigration) are no longer interested in the Buddha Dharma and will never want to realize it. Therefore, Mañjuśrī, the worldly man still reacts (favourably) to the Buddha Dharma whereas the śrāvaka does not. Why? Because when the worldly man hears about the Buddha Dharma, he can set his mind on the quest of the supreme path, thereby preserving for ever the Three Treasures (of Buddha, Dharma and Saṅgha), whereas the śrāvaka, even if he passes his lifetime listening to the Dharma and witnessing the fearlessness of the Buddha, etc., will never dream of the supreme way."

A Bodhisattva called Universal Manifestation who was present asked Vimalakīrti: "Who are your parents, wife and children, relatives and kinsmen, official and private friends, and where are your pages and maids, elephants and horse carts?"

[1] The five deadly sins: see p. 25, n. 3 for detailed explanation.

In reply Vimalakīrti chanted the following:

"Wisdom-perfection[1] is a Bodhisattva's
Mother, his father is expedient method,[2]
For the teachers of all living beings come
Only from these two (upāya and prajñā).
His wife is joy in Dharma's law;
Kindness and pity are his daughters,
His sons morality and truthfulness,
Absolute voidness his quiet abode.
Passions are his disciples
Whom he transforms at will.
Bodhipākṣita dharma[3] are his friends
Helping him to win supreme enlightenment.
All other perfections[4] are his companions.
The four winning methods[5] are his courtesans,
Hymns, chants and intonations
Of Dharma are his melodies.
Complete control over passions[6] is his park,
Passionlessness is his grove.
The (seven) grades of bodhi[7] are the flowers
Bearing the fruit of wisdom's liberation.
The pool of eightfold liberation[8]
Holds calm water which is clear and full.

[1] Wisdom perfection or prajñā-pāramitā, the sixth of the six perfections. See p. 1, n. 1.

[2] Expedient method (upāya): see p. 15, n. 1.

[3] Bodhipākṣita Dharma or the thirty-seven conditions contributory to enlightenment, see p. 10, nn. 4-5 and p. 11, nn. 1-6.

[4] The six perfections or pāramitās: see p. 1, n. 1.

[5] The four Bodhisattva winning actions (catuḥ-saṁgraha-vastu): see p. 10, n. 2.

[6] Dhāraṇī, entire control over good and evil passions and influences.

[7] The seven degrees of enlightenment (saptabodhyaṅga): see p. 1, n. 5.

[8] Liberation in eight forms (aṣṭa-vimokṣa): see p. 24, n. 1.

The seven blossoms of purity[1] are well
Arranged to bathe this undefiled (Bodhisattva) man
Whose five supernatural powers[2] are walking elephants
And horses while the Mahāyāna is his vehicle
Which, controlled by the one mind,
Rolls through the eight noble paths.[3]
(Thirty-two) distinctive marks dignify his body
While (eighty) excellences add to it their grace.
Shamefulness is his raiment
And deep mind his coiffure.
The seven riches[4] that he owns are his assets
Which, used to teach others, earn more dividends.
Dedicating all merits (to Buddhahood), his practice
Of the Dharma as received wins far greater profit.
The four dhyānas[5] are his meditation
Bed which from pure living originates.
Much learning increases wisdom
Announcing self-awakening.
His broth is the flavour of release.
The precepts are his perfumed
Salve and pure mind is his bath.
By killing the culprit kleśa
Is his boldness unsurpassed.
By defeating the four demons[6]
He plants his triumphant banner as a bodhimaṇḍala.

[1] Purity in the precepts, in the heart, in views, in doubt-discrimination, in judgement, in intellection and in nirvāṇa.

[2] The first *five* of six supernatural powers: see p. 19, n. 1.

[3] The eight noble paths (aṣṭa-mārga): see p. 11, n. 6.

[4] The seven riches are: 1, reverent listening to the Dharma; 2, faith; 3, discipline; 4, meditation; 5, zeal and devotion; 6, abnegation; and 7, shame.

[5] The four dhyāna concentrations leading to the four heavenly regions.

[6] The four demons of kleśa, of the five aggregates, of mortality and the heavenly demon.

Though he knows there is neither birth nor death
He is reborn to show himself to all,
Appearing in many countries
Like the sun seen by everyone.
When making offerings to countless
Buddhas in the ten directions
He does not discriminate
Between himself and them.
Although he knows that Buddha lands
Are void like living beings
He goes on practising the Pure Land
(Dharma) to teach and convert men.
In their kinds, features,
Voices and bearing
This fearless Bodhisattva
Can appear the same as they.
He knows the mischief demons do
But appears as one of them
Using wise expedient means
To look like them at will.
Or he appears old, ill and dying
To make living beings realize
That all things are but illusion,
To free them from all handicaps.
Or he shows the aeon's end
With fire destroying heaven and earth
So that those clinging to permanence
Realize the impermanence of things.
Then countless living beings
Call on this Bodhisattva,
Inviting him to their homes
To convert them to the Buddha path.
In heterodox books, spells,

Skills, magic, arts and talents,
He appears to be an expert
To help and benefit (all) living beings.
Appearing in their midst, he joins the Saṅgha
In order to release them from defilement
To prevent their slipping into heresy.
Then is he seen as the sun, moon or heaven[1]
As Brahmā[2] or the lord of (all) the world,[3]
At times as earth or water
Or as the wind and fire.[4]
When they fall ill or epidemics
Rage, he prepares medicinal herbs
For them to take to cure
Their illness or infection.
When famine prevails
He makes food and drink
To save them from thirst and hunger
Before teaching them the Dharma.
In times of war he teaches
Kindliness and pity
To convert living beings
So that they can live in peace.
When armies line up for battle
He gives equal strength to both.
With his authority and power, he forces
Them to be reconciled and live in harmony.
To all countries
Where there are hells

[1] At the beginning of a new aeon when obscurity prevails, he would appear as the sun or the moon to give light.

[2] Brahmā is the father of all living beings.

[3] One of the kings of the four dhyāna heavens.

[4] He appears as the wind to blow on and freeze water into earth, or as earth to rescue those drowned in water.

He comes unexpectedly
To relieve their sufferings.
Wherever animals
Devour one another
He appears among them
Urging them to do good.
Seeming to have the five desires[1]
He is always meditating
To upset the demons
And prevent their mischief.
Like that thing most rare, a lotus
Blossoming in a scorching fire,
He meditates amidst desires,
Which also is a thing most rare.
Or he appears as a prostitute
To entice those who to lust are given.
First using temptation to hook them
He then leads them to the Buddha wisdom.
He appears as a district magistrate,
Or as a chief of the caste of traders,
A state preceptor or high official
To protect living beings.
To the poor and destitute
He appears with boundless purse
To advise and guide them until
They develop the bodhi mind.
To the proud and arrogant
He appears as powerful
To overcome their vanity
'Till they tread the path supreme.
Then he comes to comfort
People who are cowards,

[1] The five desires: see p. 83, n. 1.

First he makes them fearless
Then urges them to seek the truth.
Or he appears without desires and acts
Like a seer with five spiritual powers
To convert living beings by teaching them
Morality, patience and pity.
To those needing support and help
He may appear as a servant
To please and induce them
To grow the Tao mind
Providing them with all they need
To enter on the Buddha path;
Thus using expedient methods
To supply them with all their needs.
Then as with boundless truth
His deeds are also endless;
With his wisdom that has no limit
He frees countless living beings.
If all the Buddhas were
To spend countless aeons
In praising his merits
They could never count them fully.
Who, after hearing this Dharma,
Develops not the bodhi mind,
Can only be a worthless man,
A jackass without wisdom."

CHAPTER NINE

Initiation Into the Non-dual Dharma[1]

THEREAT, Vimalakīrti said to the Bodhisattvas present: "Virtuous Ones, each of you please say something about the non-dual Dharma as you understand it."

In the meeting a Bodhisattva called "Comfort in the Dharma" said: "Virtuous Ones, birth and death are a duality but nothing is created and nothing is destroyed. Realization of this patient endurance leading to the uncreate is initiation into the non-dual Dharma."

The Bodhisattva called "Guardian of the Three Virtues"[2] said: "Subject and object are a duality for where there is ego there is also (its) object, but since fundamentally there is no ego, its object does not arise; this is initiation into the non-dual Dharma."

The Bodhisattva "Never Winking"[3] said: "Responsiveness (vedanā, the second aggregate) and unresponsiveness are a duality. If there is no response to phenomena, the latter cannot be found anywhere; hence there is neither accepting nor rejecting (of anything), and neither karmic activity nor discrimination; this is initiation into the non-dual Dharma."

The Bodhisattva "Highest virtue" said: "Impurity and

[1] i.e. the absolute state or Bhūtatathāthatā free from dualities, relativities and contraries.

[2] The three virtues or powers: the virtue or potency of the Buddha's Dharmakāya; of his prajñā or wisdom; and of his sovereign freedom.

[3] This Bodhisattva never winked because of his intense reverence to the three Treasures of Buddha, Dharma and Saṅgha.

purity are a duality. When the underlying nature of impurity is clearly perceived, even purity ceases to arise. Hence this cessation (of the idea of purity) is initiation into the non-dual Dharma."

The Bodhisattva "Winner of Samādhi by Looking at the Star" said: "(External) disturbance and (inner) thinking are a duality; when disturbance subsides, thinking comes to an end and the absence of thought leads to non-discriminating; reaching this state is initiation into the non-dual Dharma."

The Bodhisattva "Skilful Eye"[1] said: "Monistic form[2] and formlessness are a duality. If monistic form is realized as (fundamentally) formless, with relinquishment of formlessness in order to achieve impartiality, this is initiation into the non-dual Dharma."

The Bodhisattva "Wonderful Arm"[3] said: "The Bodhisattva mind and the śrāvaka mind are a duality. If the mind is looked into as void and illusory, there is neither Bodhisattva mind nor śrāvaka mind; this is initiation into the non-dual Dharma."

The Bodhisattva Puṣya[4] said: "Good and evil are a duality; if neither good nor evil arises so that formlessness is realized to attain Reality, this is initiation into the non-dual Dharma."

The Bodhisattva Siṁha (Lion) said: "Weal and woe are a duality; if the underlying nature of woe is understood, woe does not differ from weal. If the diamond (indestructible) wisdom is used to look into this with neither bondage nor

[1] i.e. the eye of wisdom.

[2] Monistic form: a Mahāyāna term which means the One Mind that creates all things.

[3] A Bodhisattva who used "the wonderful arm" of expedient method (upāya) to preach the Dharma.

[4] The twenty-third stellar mansion under the influence of which this Bodhisattva was born.

liberation (coming into play), this is initiation into the non-dual Dharma."

The Bodhisattva "Lion's Fearlessness" said: "The mundane and supramundane are a duality. If all things are looked into impartially, neither the mundane nor the supramundane will arise, with no differentiation between form and formlessness, this is initiation into the non-dual Dharma."

The Bodhisattva "Pure Interpretation" said: "Activity (ju wei) and non-activity (wu wei) are a duality, but if the mind is kept from all mental conditions it will be (void) like space and pure and clean wisdom will be free from all obstructions. This is initiation into the non-dual Dharma."

The Bodhisattva Nārāyaṇa[1] said: "The mundane and the supramundane are a duality but the underlying nature of the mundane is void (or immaterial) and is but the supramundane which can be neither entered nor left and neither overflows (like the stream of transmigration) nor scatters (like smoke). This is initiation into the non-dual Dharma."

The Bodhisattva "Skilful Mind" said: "Saṁsāra[2] and nirvāṇa are a duality. If the underlying nature of saṁsāra is perceived there exists neither birth nor death, neither bondage nor liberation, and neither rise nor fall. Such an understanding is initiation into the non-dual Dharma."

The Bodhisattva "Direct Insight"[3] said: "The exhaustible and the inexhaustible are a duality.[4] If all things are looked

[1] Nārāyaṇa: a Bodhisattva of firm and stable determination.

[2] Saṁsāra: the state of birth and death.

[3] Direct insight or direct reasoning as contrasted with comparison and inference, comparison of the known and inference of the unknown.

[4] If kleśa is cut off saṁsāra will come to an end; this is the exhaustion of all phenomena. If kleśa is not cut off and saṁsāra does not end, this is inexhaustion of phenomena. Further, impermanence will eventually come to an end; this is the exhaustible; and the Buddha-nature, inherent in all men, will never come to an end; this is the inexhaustible.

into exhaustively, both the exhaustible and the inexhaustible cannot be exhausted; and the inexhaustible is identical with the void which is beyond both the exhaustible and the inexhaustible. Such an interpretation is initiation into the non-dual Dharma."

The Bodhisattva "Upholder of Universality" said: "The ego and non-ego are a duality. Since the ego cannot be found, where can the non-ego be found? He who perceives the real nature of the ego will not give rise to dualities; this is initiation into the non-dual Dharma."

The Bodhisattva "Lightning Perception" said: "Enlightenment and unenlightenment are a duality, but the underlying nature of unenlightenment is enlightenment which should also be cast away; if all relativities are discarded and replaced by non-dual impartiality, this is initiation into the non-dual Dharma."

The Bodhisattva Priyadarśana[1] said: "Form (rūpa) and voidness are a duality, (but) form is identical with voidness, which does not mean that form wipes out voidness, for the underlying nature of form is void of itself. So are (the other four aggregates) reception (vedanā), conception (sañjñā), discrimination (saṁskāra) and consciousness (vijñāna—in relation to voidness).

"Consciousness and voidness are a duality (yet) consciousness is identical with voidness, which does not mean that consciousness wipes out voidness for the underlying nature of voidness is void of itself. A thorough understanding of this is initiation into the non-dual Dharma."

The Bodhisattva "Understanding the Four Elements" said: "The four elements (earth, water, fire and air) and their voidness are a duality (but) the underlying nature of the four elements is identical with that of voidness. Like the past

[1] Priyadarśana is a Bodhisattva whom all beings are joyful to see.

(before the four elements came into being) and the future (when they scatter away) which are both void, the present (when they appear) is also void. Identical understanding of the underlying nature of all four elements is initiation into the non-dual Dharma."

The Bodhisattva "Deep Thought" said: "Eye and form are a duality (but) if the underlying nature of the eye is known with neither desire nor anger nor stupidity in relation to things seen, this is nirvāṇa.

"Likewise, the ear and sound, the nose and smell, the tongue and taste, the body and touch, and the mind and ideation are dualities (but) if the underlying nature of the mind is known with neither desire, anger and stupidity in relation to things (heard, smelt, tasted, touched and thought), this is nirvāṇa. Resting in this state (of nirvāṇa) is initiation into the non-dual Dharma."

The Bodhisattva "Inexhaustible Mind"[1] said: "Charity-perfection (dāna-pāramitā) and the dedication (pariṇāmanā) of its merits towards realizing the all-knowledge (sarvajña) are a duality,[2] (but) the underlying nature of charity is dedication towards the All-knowledge.

"Likewise, discipline perfection (śīla-pāramitā), patience-perfection, (kṣānti-pāramitā), zeal-perfection (vīrya-pāramitā), meditation-perfection (dhyāna-pāramitā) and wisdom-perfection (prajñā-pāramitā), with dedication to the All-

[1] Inexhaustible Mind or Akṣayamati, the name of a Bodhisattva who developed an unending mind in the practice of the six endless pāramitās.

[2] Dedication (pariṇāmanā) here is somewhat similar to supererogation in the West but differs from it in that all merits derived from the practice of charity-perfection are dedicated to the final realization of the Buddha's All-knowledge for the welfare of all living beings. Merits which are not so dedicated result only in self-enlightenment in the stages of śrāvakas and pratyeka-buddhas. Mahāyāna forsakes all merits in order to realize the absolute Bhūtatathatā which is free from dualities, relativities and contraries.

knowledge, are (five) dualities, but their underlying natures are but dedication to the All-knowledge, while realization of their oneness[1] is initiation into the non-dual Dharma."

The Bodhisattva "Profound Wisdom" said: "Voidness, formlessness and non-activity[2] are (three different gates to liberation, and when each is compared to the other two there are) three dualities, (but) voidness is formless and formlessness is non-active. For when voidness, formlessness and non-activity obtain, there is neither mind, nor intellect nor consciousness, and liberation through either one of these three gates is identical with liberation through all the three. This is initiation into the non-dual Dharma."

The Bodhisattva "Unstirred Sense Organs" said: "Buddha, Dharma and Saṅgha are three different treasures and when each is compared to the other two there are three dualities (but) Buddha is identical with Dharma, and Dharma is identical with Saṅgha. For the three treasures are non-active (wu wei) and are equal to space, with the same equality for all things. The realization of this (equality) is initiation into the non-dual Dharma."

The Bodhisattva "Unimpeded Mind" said: "Body and its eradication (in nirvāṇa)[3] are a duality but body is identical with nirvāṇa. Why? Because if the underlying nature of body is perceived, no conception of (existing) body and its nirvāṇic condition will arise, for both are fundamentally non-dual, not being two different things. The absence of alarm and dread when confronting this ultimate state is initiation into the non-dual Dharma."

[1] i.e. All in One and One in All.

[2] The three gates to nirvāṇa: see p. 22, n. 1.

[3] While all worldly men regard body as real and the śrāvakas seek its extinction to realize relative nirvāṇa, the Bodhisattva looks into the underlying nature of both body and nirvāṇa to realize the non-dual Dharma in the absolute state of suchness (bhūtatathatā).

The Bodhisattva "Superior Virtue"[1] said: "The three karmas (produced by) body, mouth and mind (are different when each is compared to the other two and make three) dualities (but) their underlying nature is non-active; so non-active body is identical with non-active mouth, which is identical with non-active mind. These three karmas being non-active, all things are also non-active. Likewise, if wisdom (prajñā) is also non-active, this is initiation into the non-dual Dharma."

The Bodhisattva "Field of Blessedness"[2] said: "Good conduct, evil conduct and motionlessness[3] are (different and when each is compared to the other two make three) dualities (but) the underlying nature of all three is voidness which is free from good, evil and motionlessness. The non-rising of these three is initiation into the non-dual Dharma."

The Bodhisattva "Majestic Blossom"[4] said: "The ego and its objective are a duality, (but) if the underlying nature of the ego is looked into, this duality vanishes. If duality is cast away there will be no consciousness, and freedom from consciousness is initiation into the non-dual Dharma."

The Bodhisattva "Treasure of Threefold Potency"[5] said: "Realization implies subject and object which are a duality, but if nothing is regarded as realization, there will be neither

[1] This Bodhisattva purified the three karmas of deed, word and thought and achieved the "mean", hence his name.

[2] This Bodhisattva discarded both weal and woe to look into absolute reality and passed his life converting people to the Dharma, hence his name "Field of Blessedness" that saved all living beings.

[3] The ten good deeds result in rebirth in the higher worlds of desire, the ten evil deeds result in rebirth in the lower worlds of desire, and motionless deeds, i.e. meditation on error and its remedy, result in rebirth in the world of form and formlessness.

[4] This Bodhisattva is so called because of his practice which embellishes the flower that bears the Buddha-fruit.

[5] The potency of the Buddha's Dharmakāya, of his wisdom and of his sovereign liberty.

grasping nor rejecting, and freedom from grasping and rejecting is initiation into the non-dual Dharma."

The Bodhisattva "Moon in Midheaven"[1] said: "Darkness and light are a duality. Where there is neither darkness nor light,[2] this duality is no more. Why? Because in the state of samādhi resulting from the complete extinction of sensation and thought[3] there is neither darkness nor light, while all things disappear. A disinterested entry into this state is initiation into the non-dual Dharma."

The Bodhisattva Ratna Mudrā[4] (Precious Symbol) said: "Joy in nirvāṇa and sadness in saṁsāra are a duality which vanishes when there is no longer joy and sadness. Why? Because where there is bondage, there is also (desire for) liberation, but if fundamentally there is no bondage, who seeks liberation? Where there is neither bondage nor liberation, there will be neither joy nor sadness; this is initiation into the non-dual Dharma."

The Bodhisattva "Gem on the Head"[5] said: "Orthodoxy and heterodoxy are a duality, (but) he who dwells in (i.e. realizes) orthodoxy does not discriminate between orthodoxy and heterodoxy. Keeping from these two extremes is initiation into the non-dual Dharma."

The Bodhisattva "Joy in Reality" said: "Reality and unreality are a duality, (but) he who realizes reality does not

[1] A Bodhisattva whose wisdom is bright like the moon shining in mid-heaven.

[2] Darkness stands for unenlightenment and light for enlightenment; both are two extremes but in the absolute state there is neither unenlightenment nor enlightenment.

[3] Sensation and thought, or vedanā and sañjñā, the second and third of the five aggregates.

[4] A Bodhisattva who realized this ratna-mudrā samādhi in which he perceived the unreality of the ego and the impermanence of all things, including relative nirvāṇa.

[5] A Bodhisattva who wore reality as a gem in his head-dress, hence his name.

even perceive it, still less unreality. Why? Because reality is invisible to the ordinary eyes and appears only to the eye of wisdom. Thus (realization of) the eye of wisdom, which is neither observant nor unobservant, is initiation into the non-dual Dharma."

After the Bodhisattvas had spoken, they asked Mañjuśrī for his opinion on the non-dual Dharma.

Mañjuśrī said: "In my opinion, when all things are no longer within the province of either word or speech, and of either indication or knowledge, and are beyond questions and answers, this is initiation into the non-dual Dharma."

Thereat, Mañjuśrī asked Vimalakīrti: "All of us have spoken; please tell us what is the Bodhisattva's initiation into the non-dual Dharma."

Vimalakīrti kept silent without saying a word.

At that, Mañjuśrī exclaimed: "Excellent, excellent; can there be true initiation into the non-dual Dharma until words and speech are no longer written or spoken?[1]

After this initiation into the non-dual Dharma had been expounded, five thousand Bodhisattvas at the meeting were initiated into it thereby realizing the patient endurance of the uncreate.

[1] Mañjuśrī still spoke of words, speech, indication, knowledge, questions and answers, but Vimalakīrti even wiped out all traces of them to reveal the true initiation into the absolute.

CHAPTER TEN

The Buddha of the Fragrant Land

ŚĀRIPUTRA was thinking of mealtime and of the food for the Bodhisattvas in the meeting when Vimalakīrti, who read his thought, said to him: "The Buddha taught the eight forms of liberation which you have received for practice; do you now mix your desire to eat with His Dharma? If you want to eat, please wait for a moment and you will have a rare treat."

At that, Vimalakīrti entered the state of samādhi and used his transcendental power to show to the assembly a country which is above, separated from this world by a distance represented by Buddha lands as countless as sand grains in forty-two Ganges rivers and which was called the country of All Fragrances, whose Buddha was called the Tathāgata of the Fragrant Land, and was still there. The fragrance of that country surpassed all scents emitted by the devas in Buddha lands in the ten directions. In that Buddha land there were neither śrāvakas nor pratyeka-buddhas but only pure and clean Bodhisattvas to whom that Buddha expounded the Dharma. All things there are formed by fragrances, such as palaces, the earth, gardens and parks which emit sweet scent, and the fragrance of its food spreads to countless worlds in the ten directions. Its Buddha and Bodhisattvas were sitting down for the meal offered to them by the sons of devas who were all called Glorious Fragrances,[1]

[1] Their minds were set on meditating on that Buddha and became permeated and glorified by his fragrance and light.

and were setting their minds on the quest of supreme enlightenment. This was seen by all those present in the meeting.

Vimalakīrti said to his listeners: "Virtuous Ones, who of you can go there to beg for food from that Buddha?"

As Mañjuśrī was noted for his supernatural power, all the Bodhisattvas kept silent. Thereat, Vimalakīrti said: "Are not the Virtuous Ones ashamed (of their inability to do so)?"

Mañjuśrī retorted: "As the Buddha has said, those who have not yet studied (and practised) Mahāyāna should not be slighted."[1]

Thereupon, Vimalakīrti, without rising from his seat, used his transcendental power to create an illusory (bogus) Bodhisattva whose features were radiant and whose dignity was unsurpassable, overshadowing the whole assembly. He then said to this illusory Bodhisattva: "Ascend to the Fragrant Land to call on its Buddha, saying what I now tell you: 'Upāsaka Vimalakīrti bows his head at your feet to pay his reverence and enquires respectfully about your happy tidings; he hopes you are well and have no difficulties (in converting living beings) and that your vigour is in full. He wishes to receive some leftovers from your meal to do the salvation work in the sahā world for the purpose of converting to Mahāyāna those of the small vehicle and of spreading the renown of the Tathāgata to make it known everywhere'."

After that, the illusory Bodhisattva ascended and was seen by the whole assembly to approach the Buddha of Fragrance land and repeat what Vimalakīrti had ordered

[1] The Buddha meant that all living beings possess the Buddha-nature and can win liberation if they hear and practise the Dharma.

For ethical reasons, Mañjuśrī did not interfere with Vimalakīrti's work of salvation and did not come forward in response to the upāsaka's challenge. Hence this sūtra is called "A sūtra spoken by Vimalakīrti".

him to say. When the Bodhisattvas there saw the messenger, they praised the rare visit, asking their Buddha: "Where does this Bodhisattva come from? Where is this world called sahā? What does the small vehicle mean?"

Their Buddha replied: "There is a world called sahā which is below and is separated from here by Buddha lands as countless as the sand grains in forty-two Ganges rivers, whose Buddha is called Śākyamuni and is now staying in the midst of five turbid conditions,[1] where he teaches the supreme Dharma to those clinging to the small vehicle. Over there is a Bodhisattva called Vimalakīrti who has achieved inconceivable liberation and is expounding the Dharma to other (young) Bodhisattvas. Hence he has created an illusory messenger to extol my name and praise this land so that they can earn more merits."

The Bodhisattvas asked: "Who is that Bodhisattva who can create an illusory messenger and whose transcendental powers, fearlessness and ubiquity are so great?"

That Buddha replied: "His (powers, fearlessness and ubiquity) are very great indeed. He used to send his illusory messengers to all places in the ten directions to perform the Bodhisattva work of salvation for the benefit of living beings."

That Buddha then filled a bowl of fragrant rice and handed it to the illusory messenger. All his nine million Bodhisattvas declared they all wished to go to sahā to pay reverence to Śākyamuni Buddha and to see Vimalakīrti and the other Bodhisattvas there.

That Buddha warned them: "You may go there but hide your fragrance lest the people give rise to the wrong

[1] See *The Śūraṅgama Sūtra*, p. 105, n. 1 (Rider, London) for a detailed explanation of the five conditions of turbidity: turbid aeon, turbid views, turbid passion, turbid being and turbid life.

thought of clinging to it. You should also change your appearance in order not to provoke their self-abasement. To avoid wrong views do not slight them. Why? Because all worlds in the ten directions are (fundamentally immaterial) like space and because all Buddhas wishing to convert those of the small vehicle do not reveal completely to them their own pure and clean lands."

At that, the illusory messenger received the bowl of fragrant rice and together with the nine million Bodhisattvas availed themselves of that Buddha's and Vimalakīrti's transcendental powers, disappeared from the fragrant land and, a little later, arrived at Vimalakīrti's abode.

Vimalakīrti then used his transcendental powers to make nine million lion thrones as majestic as those already there, for the visitors. The illusory messenger then handed him the bowl of rice the fragrance of which spread to the whole town of Vaiśālī and then to the whole great chiliocosm.

Brahmin devotees at Vaiśālī perceived the fragrance and became elated; they praised the rare occurrence. Their chief, called "Lunar Canopy" took eighty-four thousand men to Vimalakīrti's house where they saw many Bodhisattvas seated on majestic lion thrones; they were jubilant and paid reverence to the Bodhisattvas and the Buddha's chief disciples, and then stood at one side. Earthly and heavenly ghosts as well as the devas of the worlds of desire and of form who smelt the fragrance, came as well.

Thereat, Vimalakīrti said to Śāriputra and the śrāvakas: "Virtuous Ones, you may now take the Tathāgata's immortal rice which has been infused with great compassion; do not give rise to the thought of limitation when taking it or you will not be able to digest it."

When some śrāvakas thought that the small quantity of rice seemed insufficient for the whole assembly, the illusory

Bodhisattva said: "Do not use the little virtue and intelligence of a śrāvaka to estimate the Tathāgata's boundless blessedness and wisdom; the four oceans are exhaustible but this rice is inexhaustible. If all men took and rolled it into a ball as large as (Mount) Sumeru, they would not have finished eating it by the end of the aeon. Why? Because food that has been left over by those who have practised boundless morality and discipline (śīla), serenity (dhyāna) and wisdom (prajñā), liberation and knowledge of liberation,[1] and who have won all merits, is inexhaustible; hence this bowl of rice will satisfy the whole meeting without being exhausted. The Bodhisattvas, śrāvakas, devas and men who take it will experience comfort and joy, like the Bodhisattvas of all blessed pure lands. Their pores will give out profound fragrance which is like the scent of the trees in fragrant lands."

Vimalakīrti then asked the visiting Bodhisattvas: "How does the Tathāgata of your land preach the Dharma?"

They replied: "The Tathāgata of our land does not use word and speech to preach but uses the various fragrances to stimulate the devas in their observance of the commandments. They sit under fragrant trees and perceive how sweet the trees smell thereby realizing the samādhi derived from the store of all merits. When they realize this samādhi, they win all merits."

These Bodhisattvas then asked Vimalakīrti: "How does the World Honoured One, Śākyamuni Buddha, preach the Dharma?"

Vimalakīrti replied: "Living beings of this world are pig-headed and difficult to convert; hence the Buddha uses strong language to tame them. He speaks of hells, animals and hungry ghosts in their planes of suffering; of the places

[1] Knowledge and personal experience of all stages of enlightenment in order to avoid mistaking any of the preliminary degrees for the ultimate one.

of rebirth for stupid men as retribution for perverse deeds, words and thoughts, i.e. for killing, stealing, carnality, lying, double tongue, coarse language, affected speech, covetousness, anger, perverted views (which are the ten evils); for stinginess, breaking the precepts, anger, remissness, confused thoughts and stupidity (i.e. the six hindrances to the six pāramitās); for accepting, observing and breaking the prohibitions; for things that should and should not be done; for obstructions and non-obstructions; for what is sinful and what is not; for purity and filthines; for the worldly and holy states; for heterodoxy and orthodoxy; for activity and non-activity; and for saṁsāra and nirvāṇa. Since the minds of those who are difficult to convert are like monkeys, various methods of preaching are devised to check them so that they can be entirely tamed. Like elephants and horses which cannot be tamed without whipping them until they feel pain and become easily managed, the stubborn of this world can be disciplined only with bitter and eager words."

After hearing this, the visiting Bodhisattvas said: "We have never heard of the World Honoured One, Śākyamuni Buddha, who conceals his boundless sovereign power to appear as a beggar to mix with those who are poor in order to win their confidence (for the purpose of liberating them) and of the Bodhisattvas here who are indefatigable and so humble and whose boundless compassion caused their rebirth in this Buddha land."

Vimalakīrti said: "As you have said, the Bodhisattvas of this world have strong compassion, and their lifelong works of salvation for all living beings surpass those done in other pure lands during hundreds and thousands of aeons. Why? Because they achieved ten excellent deeds which are not required in other pure lands. What are these ten excellent deeds? They are: 1, charity (dāna) to succour the poor; 2, precept-keeping (śīla) to help those who have broken the commandments; 3, patient endurance (kṣānti) to subdue their anger; 4, zeal and devotion (vīrya) to cure their remissness; 5, serenity (dhyāna) to stop their confused thoughts; 6, wisdom (prajñā) to wipe out ignorance; 7, putting an end to the eight distressful conditions[1] for those suffering from them; 8, teaching Mahāyāna to those who cling to Hīnayāna; 9, cultivation of good roots for those in want of merits; and 10, the four Bodhisattva winning devices[2] for the purpose of leading all living beings to their goals (in Bodhisattva development). These are the ten excellent deeds."

The visiting Bodhisattvas asked: "How many Dharmas should a Bodhisattva achieve in this world to stop its morbid growth (defilements) in order to be reborn in the Buddha's pure land?"

Vimalakīrti replied: "A Bodhisattva should bring to perfection eight Dharmas to stop morbid growth in this world in order to be reborn in the pure land. They are: 1, benevolence towards all living beings with no expectation of reward; 2, endurance of sufferings for all living beings dedicating all merits to them; 3, impartiality towards them with all humility free from pride and arrogance; 4, reverence to all Bodhisattvas with the same devotion as to all Buddhas (i.e. without discrimination between Bodhisattvas and Buddhas); 5, absence of doubt and suspicion when hearing (the expounding of) sūtras which he has not heard before; 6, abstention from opposition to the śrāvaka Dharma;[3] 7,

[1] The eight distressful conditions in which it is difficult to meet a Buddha or hear the Dharma: see p. 11, n. 7.

[2] The four Bodhisattva winning devices (catuḥ-saṁgrahan-vastu): see p. 10, n. 2.

[3] The śrāvaka Dharma was also taught by the Buddha before His revelation of Mahāyāna.

abstention from discrimination in regard to donations and offerings received with no thought of self-profit in order to subdue his mind; and 8, self-examination without contending with others. Thus he should achieve singleness of mind bent on achieving all merits; these are the eight Dharmas."

After Vimalakīrti and Mañjuśrī had thus expounded the Dharma, hundreds and thousands of devas developed the mind set on supreme enlightenment, and ten thousand Bodhisattvas realized the patient endurance of the uncreate.

CHAPTER ELEVEN

The Bodhisattva Conduct

THE Buddha was expounding the Dharma at Āmravana park which suddenly became majestic and extensive while all those present turned golden hued.

Ānanda asked the Buddha: "World Honoured One, what is the cause of these auspicious signs, why does this place become extensive and majestic and why does the assembly turn golden hued?"

The Buddha replied: "This is because Vimalakīrti and Mañjuśrī, with their followers circumambulating them, want to come here; hence these auspicious signs."

(At Vaiśālī) Vimalakīrti said to Mañjuśrī: "We can now go and see the Buddha, so that we and the Bodhisattvas can pay reverence and make offerings to Him."

Mañjuśrī said: "Excellent, let us go; it is now time to start."

Vimalakīrti then used his transcendental powers to carry the whole meeting with the lion thrones on the palm of his right hand and flew (in the air) to the Buddha's place. When they landed there, Vimalakīrti bowed his head at His feet, walked round Him from the right seven times, and bringing his palms together, stood at one side. The Bodhisattvas left their lion thrones to bow their heads at His feet, and also walked round Him seven times and stood at one side. The Buddha's chief disciples with Indra, Brahmā (both as protectors of the Dharma) and the four deva kings of the four heavens, also left their lion thrones, bowed their heads at His feet, walked round Him seven times and then stood at one side.

The Buddha comforted the Bodhisattvas and ordered them to take their seats to listen to His teaching. After they had sat down, the Buddha asked Śāriputra: "Have you seen what the great Bodhisattvas have done with their transcendental powers?" Śāriputra replied that he had and He asked: "What do you think of all this?" Śāriputra answered: "I saw them do inconceivable (feats) which the mind can neither think of nor estimate."

Ānanda then asked the Buddha: "World Honoured One, the fragrance we are smelling was never perceived before; what is it?"

The Buddha replied: "Ānanda, it is the fragrance given out by the pores of these Bodhisattvas."

At that, Śāriputra said to Ānanda: "Our pores also give the same fragrance."

Ānanda asked Śāriputra: "Where does it come from?"

Śāriputra replied: "It is this upāsaka Vimalakīrti who obtained what was left over from the Buddha's meal in the Fragrant Land, and those who ate it at his abode give out this fragrance from their pores."

Ānanda then asked Vimalakīrti: "How long does this fragrance last?"

Vimalakīrti replied: "It lasts until the rice has been digested."

Ānanda asked: "How long does this take?"

Vimalakīrti replied: "It will be digested after a week. Ānanda, śrāvakas who have not reached the right position (nirvāṇa) will attain it after taking this rice which will then be digestible, and those who have attained nirvāṇa will realize liberation of their minds (from the subtle conception of nirvāṇa) and then the rice will be digested. Those who have not developed the Mahāyāna mind will develop it and then the rice will be digested. Those who have developed it and take this rice will achieve the patient endurance of the uncreate, and the rice will then be digestible. Those who have achieved the patient endurance of the uncreate and take this rice will reincarnate once more for final development into Buddhahood and the rice will be digested.[1] Like an efficacious medicine which cures an ailment before wasting away, this rice will be digestible after it has killed all troubles and afflictions (kleśa)."

Ānanda said to the Buddha: "World Honoured One, it is indeed a rare thing that this fragrant rice performs the Buddha work of salvation."

The Buddha said: "It is so, Ānanda, it is so. There are Buddha lands where the Buddha light performs the work of salvation; where the Bodhisattvas perform it; where illusory men created by the Buddha do it; where the bo-trees do it; where the Buddha's robe and bedding do it; where the rice taken by the Buddha does it; where parks and temples do it; where (the Buddha's) thirty-two physical marks[2] and their eighty notable characteristics do it; where the Buddha's body (rūpa-kāya) does it; and where empty space does it; and living beings practise discipline with success because of these causes. Also used for the same purpose are dream, illusion, shadow, echo, the image in a mirror, the moon reflected in water, the flame of a fire, sound, voice, word, speech and writing, the pure and clean Buddha land, silence

[1] A Bodhisattva passes through ten stages of development to become a Mahāsattva and the eleventh stage to become a full-fledged Buddha; it is the stage reached by Maitreya who is now in the Tuṣita heaven before coming to earth as the next Buddha.

[2] The thirty-two physical marks of a Buddha: see for detailed explanations Ch'an and Zen Teaching, First Series, p. 178, n. 2. (Rider London; Shambala, Berkeley.)

with neither word nor speech, neither pointing, discerning, action nor activity. Thus, Ānanda, whatever the Buddhas do by either revealing or concealing their awe-inspiring majesty, is the work of salvation. Ānanda, because of the four basic delusions (in reference to the ego)[1] divided into 84,000 defilements which cause living beings to endure troubles and tribulations, the Buddhas avail themselves of these trials to perform their works of salvation. This is called entering the Buddha's Dharma door to enlightenment (Dharmaparyāya).

"When entering this Dharma door, if a Bodhisattva sees all the clean Buddha lands, he should not give rise to joy, desire and pride, and if he sees all the unclean Buddha lands[2] he should not give rise to sadness, hindrance and disappointment; he should develop a pure and clean mind to revere all Tathāgatas who rarely appear and whose merits are equal in spite of their appearance in different lands (clean and unclean) to teach and convert living beings.

"Ānanda, you can see different Buddha lands (i.e. clean and unclean) but you see no difference in space which is the same everywhere. Likewise, the physical bodies of Buddhas differ from one another[3] but their omniscience is the same.

"Ānanda, the (underlying) nature of the physical bodies of the Buddhas, their discipline, serenity, liberation and full knowledge of liberation, their (ten) powers,[4] their (four) fearlessnesses,[5] their eighteen unsurpassed characteristics,[6] their boundless kindness and compassion, their dignified

[1] The four basic delusions: unenlightenment in regard to the ego; holding to the ego idea; self-esteem, egotism, pride; and self-seeking or desire.

[2] i.e. this unclean world which was the land of Śākyamuni Buddha.

[3] The material rūpa-kāya as contrasted with the immaterial Dharmakāya.

[4] The ten powers of a Buddha (daśabala): see p. 2, n. 1.

[5] The Buddha's four fearlessnesses: see p. 40, n. 6.

[6] The Buddha's eighteen unsurpassed characteristics: see p. 3, n. 1.

deeds, their infinite lives, their preaching of the Dharma to teach and convert living beings and to purify Buddha lands are all the same. Hence their titles of Samyaksambuddha,[1] Tathāgata,[2] and Buddha.[3]

"Ānanda, if I am to give you the full meaning of these three titles you will pass the whole aeon without being able to hear it completely. Even if the great chiliocosm is full of living beings who are all good listeners and like you can hold in memory everything they hear about the Dharma, they will also pass the whole aeon without being able to hear my full explanation (of these three titles). For, Ānanda, the Buddha's supreme enlightenment is boundless and his wisdom and power of speech are inconceivable."

Ānanda said: "From now on I dare no more claim to have heard much of the Dharma."

The Buddha said: "Ānanda, do not give way to back-sliding. Why? Because I have said that you have heard much more about the Dharma than the śrāvakas but not than the Bodhisattvas. Ānanda, a wise man should not make a limited estimate of the Bodhisattva stage (because) the depths of the oceans can be measured but the Bodhisattva's serenity, wisdom, imperturbability, power of speech and all his merits cannot be measured. Ānanda, let us put aside the Bodhisattva conduct. The transcendental powers which Vimalakīrti has demonstrated today cannot be achieved by all śrāvakas and pratyeka-buddhas using their spiritual powers for hundreds and thousands of aeons."

Thereat, the visiting Bodhisattvas put their palms together and said to the Buddha: "World Honoured One, when we first saw this world we thought of its inferiority

1 Samyaksambuddha: the omniscient.

2 Tathāgata: the absolute who comes as do all other Buddhas.

3 Buddha: the enlightened one.

but we now repent of our wrong opinion. Why? Because the expedients (upāya) employed by all Buddhas are inconceivable;[1] their aim being to deliver living beings they appear in different Buddha lands suitable for the purpose. World Honoured One, will you please bestow upon us some little Dharma so that when we return to our own land we can always remember you."

The Buddha said to them: "There are the exhaustible and the inexhaustible Dharmas which you should study. What is the exhaustible? It is the active (yu wei or mundane) Dharma. What is the inexhaustible? It is the non-active (wu wei or supramundane) Dharma. As Bodhisattvas, you should not exhaust (or put an end to) the mundane (state); nor should you stay in the supramundane (state).[2]

"What is meant by not exhausting the mundane (state)? It means not discarding great benevolence; not abandoning great compassion; developing a profound mind set on the quest of all-knowledge (sarvajña or Buddha knowledge) without relaxing for even an instant; indefatigable teaching and converting living beings; constant practice of the four Bodhisattva winning methods;[3] upholding the right Dharma even at the risk of one's body and life; unwearied planting

[1] i.e. the expedient device which shows the Fragrant Land and its fragrant rice to urge those who see them to set their minds on the quest of inconceivable liberation.

[2] Although the mundane or causative state is false, if the Bodhisattvas leave it they will not achieve their great work of salvation; and although the supramundane or non-causative state is Reality, if they dwell in it their wisdom will be incomplete for this is self-enlightenment but not universal enlightenment. For if they do not quit the worldly state they will be able to save living beings and their merits will be boundless thus overcoming all obstructions encountered by worldly men; on the other hand, if they do not stay in the supramundane state or nirvāṇa, their wisdom will be free from the duality of subject (self) and object (nirvāṇa) and will be boundless thus overcoming all hindrances encountered by Hīnayāna men.

[3] The four Bodhisattva winning devices: see p. 10, n. 2.

of all excellent roots; unceasing application of expedient devices (upāya) and dedication (pariṇāmanā);[1] never-ending quest of the Dharma; unsparing preaching of it; diligent worship of all Buddhas; hence fearlessness when entering the stream of birth and death; absence of joy in honour and of sadness in disgrace; refraining from slighting non-practisers of the Dharma;[2] respecting practisers of Dharma as if they were Buddhas; helping those suffering from kleśa to develop the right thought; keeping away from (desire and) pleasure with no idea of prizing such a high conduct; no preference for one's happiness but joy at that of others; regarding one's experience in the state of samādhi as similar to that in a hell; considering one's stay in saṁsāra (i.e. state of birth and death) as similar to a stroll in a park;[3] giving rise to the thought of being a good teacher of Dharma when meeting those seeking it; giving away all possessions to realize all-knowledge (sarvajña); giving rise to the thought of salvation when seeing those breaking the precepts; thinking of the (six) perfections (pāramitās) as dear as one's parents; thinking of the (thirty-seven) conditions contributory to enlightenment[4] as if they were one's helpful relatives; planting all excellent roots without any restrictions; gathering the glorious adornments of all pure lands to set up one's own Buddha land; unrestricted bestowal of Dharma to win all the excellent physical marks (of the Buddha);[5] wiping out all evils to purify one's body, mouth and mind; developing undiminished bravery while transmigrating through

[1] Dedication (pariṇāmanā): see p. 96, n. 2.

[2] Because they also possess the Buddha-nature and may eventually achieve enlightenment before you.

[3] Both this and the preceding sentences teach the sameness of two extremes which have no room in the absolute state.

[4] The thirty-seven conditions contributory to enlightenment: see p. 10, nn. 4-5 and p 11, nn. 1-6.

[5] The thirty-two excellent physical marks of the Buddha: see p. 11, n. 2.

saṁsāra in countless aeons; untiring determination to listen to (an account of) the Buddha's countless merits; using the sword of wisdom to destroy the bandit of kleśa (temptation) to take living beings out of (the realm of the five) aggregates (skandhas) and (twelve) entrances (āyatana) so as to liberate them for ever; using firm devotion to destroy the army of demons; unceasing search for the thought-free wisdom of reality; content with few desires while not running away from the world in order to continue the Bodhisattva work of salvation; not infringing the rules of respect-inspiring deportment while entering the world (to deliver living beings); use of the transcendental power derived from wisdom to guide and lead all living beings; controlling (dhāraṇī) the thinking process in order never to forget the Dharma; being aware of the roots of all living beings in order to cut off their doubts and suspicions (about their underlying nature); use of the power of speech to preach the Dharma without impediment; perfecting the ten good (deeds)[1] to win the blessings of men and devas (in order to be reborn among them to spread the Dharma); practising the four infinite minds (kindness, pity, joy and indifference)[2] to teach the Brahma heavens; rejoicing at being invited to expound and extol the Dharma in order to win the Buddha's (skilful) method of preaching; realizing excellence of body, mouth and mind to win the Buddha's respect-inspiring deportment; profound practice of good Dharma to make one's deeds unsurpassed; practising Mahāyāna to become a Bodhisattva monk; and developing a never-receding mind in order not to miss all excellent merits.

"This is the Bodhisattva not exhausting the mundane state.

[1] The ten good deeds are the opposites of the ten evils: see p. 84, n. 2.

[2] The four infinite minds: see p. 10, n. 1.

"What is the Bodhisattva not staying in the supramundane state (nirvāṇa)? It means studying and practising the immaterial but without abiding in voidness;[1] studying and practising formlessness and inaction but without abiding in them; studying and practising that which is beyond causes but without remaining in it; looking into impermanence without discarding the roots of good causation;[2] looking into suffering in the world without hating birth and death (i.e. saṁsāra);[3] looking into the absence of the ego while continuing to teach all living beings indefatigably;[4] looking into nirvāṇa with no intention of dwelling in it permanently;[5] looking into the relinquishment (of nirvāṇa) while one's body and mind are set on the practice of all good deeds;[6] looking into the (non-existing) destinations of all things[7] while the mind is set on practising excellent actions (as true destinations);[8] looking into the unborn (i.e. the uncreate) while abiding in (the illusion of) life to shoulder responsibility (to save others); looking into

[1] Because if one abides in voidness one will be unable to carry on the work of salvation.

[2] Although good causation is also impermanent it forms good karma which wins good merits and also contributes to realizing enlightenment.

[3] He should rise above love and hate in order to wipe out all dualities to win enlightenment.

[4] Although egolessness implies the non-existence of living beings, the Bodhisattva's indefatigable preaching is necessary for self-enlightenment and enlightenment of others.

[5] Nirvāṇa is the state of utter stillness and complete extinction of all worldly existence but a Bodhisattva does not remain in it like Hīnayāna men who only seek self-enlightenment.

[6] There are three hindrances which should be avoided: the five pleasures, kleśa and nirvāṇa. The text means the third hindrance or nirvāṇa which should be relinquished so as not to fall into the relative nirvāṇa sought by Hīnayāna men and in order to win boundless merits leading to complete enlightenment or parinirvāṇa.

[7] All things or phenomena are unreal and neither come nor go.

[8] In order to win boundless merits which contribute to the realization of enlightenment.

passionlessness without cutting off the passion-stream (in order to stay in the world to liberate others); looking into the state of non-action while carrying out the Dharma to teach and convert living beings; looking into nothingness without forgetting about great compassion; looking into the right position (i.e. nirvāṇa) without following the Hīnayāna habit (of staying in it); looking into the unreality of all phenomena which are neither firm nor have an independent nature, and are egoless and formless, but since one's own fundamental vows are not entirely fulfilled, one should not regard merits, serenity and wisdom as unreal and so cease practising them.

"This is the Bodhisattva not staying in the non-active (wu wei) state.

"Further, to win merits, a Bodhisattva does not stay in the supramundane, and to realize wisdom he does not exhaust the mundane. Because of his great kindness and compassion, he does not remain in the supramundane, and in order to fulfil all his vows, he does not exhaust the mundane. To gather the Dharma medicines he does not stay in the supramundane, and to administer remedies he does not exhaust the mundane. Since he knows the illnesses of all living beings he does not stay in the supramundane, and since he wants to cure their illnesses, he does not exhaust the mundane.

"Virtuous Ones, a Bodhisattva practising this Dharma neither exhausts the mundane nor stays in the supramundane. This is called the exhaustible and inexhaustible Dharma doors to liberation which you should study."

After hearing the Buddha expounding the Dharma, the visiting Bodhisattvas were filled with joy and rained (heavenly) flowers of various colours and fragrances in the great chiliocosm as offerings to the Buddha and His sermon.

After this, they bowed their heads at the Buddha's feet and praised His teaching which they had not heard before, saying: "How wonderful is Śākyamuni Buddha's skilful use of expedient methods (upāya)."

After saying this they disappeared to return to their own land.

CHAPTER TWELVE

Seeing Akṣobhya Buddha[1]

THE Buddha then asked Vimalakīrti: "You spoke of coming here to see the Tathāgata, but how do you see Him impartially?"[2]

Vimalakīrti replied: "Seeing reality in one's body is how to see the Buddha.[3] I see the Tathāgata did not come in the past, will not go in the future, and does not stay in the present. The Tathāgata is seen neither in form (rūpa, the first aggregate) nor in the extinction of form nor in the underlying nature of form. Neither is He seen in responsiveness (vedanā), conception (sañjñā), discrimination (saṁskāra) and consciousness (vijñāna) (i.e. the four other

[1] The fragrant land, revealed previously, was for Hīnayāna men to compare its purity to sahā's filthiness in order to stimulate them to develop the Mahāyāna mind and practise the Bodhisattva path.

This chapter reveals the pure land of Akṣobhya Buddha to teach that a land is pure when the mind is pure and is impure when the mind is corrupt, and that there is no pure land apart from this filthy world for at the time of enlightenment the pure land is *here*, *now on the spot* and not elsewhere.

[2] i.e. how do you see Him in an unprejudiced manner?—The Buddha referred to what Vimalakīrti had said to Mañjuśrī: "We can now go and *see the Buddha*" (see p. 109 fourth paragraph) and asked the upāsaka how he would see the Tathāgata.

[3] This is like going against the stream (the body) to reach its source (the Buddha-nature in man) for all things arise from the mind which, when free from bondage, is enlightenment. For reality is neither form nor formlessness, neither unity nor diversity, neither this nor that, but the distinct solitary light that is the substance of the mind which is the same in either a living being or in a Buddha. Hence "seeing reality in the body is how to see the Buddha". In other words, to see the Tathāgata, one should see into one's own mind (in one's body) which is the aim of the Ch'an teaching and the method taught by Avalokiteśvara in the Śūraṅgama Sūtra (see *The Śūraṅgama Sūtra*, p. 135 last paragraph. Rider, London).

aggregates), their extinction and their underlying natures. The Tathāgata is not created by the four elements (earth, water, fire and air) for He is (immaterial) like space. He does not come from the union of the six entrances (i.e. the six sense organs) for He is beyond eye, ear, nose, tongue, body and intellect. He is beyond the three worlds (of desire, form and formlessness) for He is free from the three defilements (desire, hate and stupidity). He is in line with the three gates to nirvāṇa[1] and has achieved the three states of enlightenment (or three insights)[2] which do not differ from (the underlying nature of) unenlightenment. He is neither unity nor diversity, neither selfness nor otherness, neither form nor formlessness,[3] neither on this shore (of unenlightenment) nor on the other shore (of enlightenment) nor in midstream[4] when converting living beings. He looks into the nirvāṇic condition (of stillness and extinction of worldly existence) but does not dwell in its permanent extinction.[5] He is neither this nor that and cannot be revealed by these two extremes.[6] He cannot be known by intellect or perceived by consciousness.[7] He is neither bright nor obscure. He is nameless and formless,[8] being neither strong nor weak, neither clean nor unclean,[9] neither in a given place nor

1 The three gates to the city of Nirvāṇa: voidness, formlessness and non-activity. See p. 22, n. 1.

2 The three states of enlightenment or three insights: see p. 19, n. 2.

3 He is free from bondage to formless nirvāṇa and to illusory form in saṁsāra.

4 He is beyond the duality of unenlightenment and enlightenment, and does not abide in the midstream in order to convert all living beings.

5 Nirvāṇa is the state of stillness and extinction of all worldly existence which cannot be subject to further extinction. Moreover, he does not dwell in nirvāṇa in order to carry on his work of salvation.

6 For he is non-dual and is absolute.

7 For it is unthinkable.

8 For he is beyond name and form, the fourth of the twelve nidānas or links in the chain of existence.

9 He is beyond all relativities and contraries.

outside of it,[1] and neither mundane nor supramundane. He can neither be pointed out nor spoken of.[2] He is neither charitable nor selfish; he neither keeps nor breaks the precepts; is beyond patience and anger, diligence and remissness, stillness and disturbance. He is neither intelligent nor stupid, and neither honest nor deceitful. He neither comes nor goes and neither enters nor leaves. He is beyond the paths of word and speech.[3] He is neither the field of blessedness nor its opposite, neither worthy nor unworthy of worship and offerings. He can be neither seized nor released and is beyond 'is' and 'is not'. He is equal to reality and to the nature of Dharma (Dharmatā) and cannot be designated and estimated, for he is beyond figuring and measuring. He is neither large nor small, is neither visible nor audible, can neither be felt nor known, is free from all ties and bondage, is equal to the All-knowledge and to the (underlying) nature of all living beings, and cannot be differentiated from all things. He is beyond gain and loss, free from defilement and troubles (kleśa), beyond creating and giving rise (to anything), beyond birth and death, beyond fear and worry, beyond like and dislike, and beyond existence in the past, future and present.[4] He cannot be revealed by word, speech, discerning and pointing.

"World Honoured One, the body of the Tathāgata being such, seeing Him as above-mentioned is correct whereas seeing Him otherwise is wrong."

[1] He is beyond space for he is omnipresent.

[2] For he is inconceivable.

[3] He has attained the stage which is inexpressible either verbally or in writing.

[4] Our translation follows the Chinese text in which the *past* is placed before the *future* which is followed by the *present* to agree with the ancient way of reasoning thus: "the past is no more, the future has not come and the present does not stay"— the past and future standing for "*is not*" and the present for "*is*".

This note is added to forestall groundless criticism to which the author has been subjected since the publication of his books because the eastern way of thinking sometimes differs from that in the west. See also p. 36, n. 1.

Thereupon, Śāriputra asked Vimalakīrti: "Where did you die to be reborn here?"[1]

Vimalakīrti asked back: "Is the (śrāvaka) Dharma which you have realized subject to death and rebirth?"[2]

Śāriputra replied: "It is beyond death and birth."

Vimalakīrti asked: "If there is neither birth nor death, why did you ask me: 'Where did you die to be reborn here?' What do you think of illusory men and women created by an illusionist; are they subject to death and birth?"

Śāriputra replied: "They are not subject to death and birth. Have you not heard the Buddha say that all things are illusions?"

Vimalakīrti said: "Yes, if all things are illusions, why did you ask me where I died to be reborn here? Śāriputra, death is unreal and deceptive, and means decay and destruction (to the worldly man), while life which is also unreal and deceptive means continuance to him. As to the Bodhisattva, although he disappears (in one place) he does not put an end to his good (deeds), and although he reappears (in another) he prevents evils from arising."[3]

Thereat, the Buddha said to Śāriputra: "There is a (Buddha) land called the realm of Profound Joy whose Buddha is Akṣobhya Buddha[4] where Vimalakīrti disappeared to come here."[5]

Śāriputra said: "It is a rare thing, World Honoured One,

[1] Śāriputra admired Vimalakīrti's power of speech and asked where he had learned all this before his rebirth at Vaiśālī.

[2] Śāriputra had realized birthlessness as taught by Hīnayāna which teaches that birth and death are illusory and false.

[3] Vimalakīrti discusses birth and death which are true to the worldly man but false to the Bodhisattva.

[4] The immutable, imperturbable and serene Buddha (in the midst of disturbance in the East).

[5] The Buddha reveals Vimalakīrti's country of origin which he left to come to Vaiśālī to deliver men.

that this man could leave a pure land to come to this world full of hatred and harmfulness!"

Vimalakīrti asked Śāriputra: "Śāriputra, what do you think of sunlight; when it appears does it unite with darkness?"

Śāriputra replied: "Where there is sunlight, there is no darkness."

Vimalakīrti asked: "Why does the sun shine on Jambudvīpa (this earth)?"

Śāriputra replied: "It shines to destroy darkness."

Vimalakīrti said: "Likewise, a Bodhisattva, although born in an unclean Buddha land, does not join and unite with the darkness of ignorance but (teaches and) converts living beings to destroy the obscurity of kleśa."

As the assembly admired and wished to see the Immutable Tathāgata, the Bodhisattvas and śrāvakas of the pure land of Profound Joy, the Buddha who read their thoughts said to Vimalakīrti: "Virtuous man, please show the Immutable Tathāgata and the Bodhisattvas and śrāvakas of the land of Profound Joy to this assembly who want to see them."

Vimalakīrti thought that he should, while remaining seated, take with his hand the world of Profound Joy with its iron enclosing mountains,[1] hills, rivers, streams, ravines, springs, seas, Sumerus, sun, moon, stars, planets, palaces of heavenly dragons, ghosts, spirits and devas, Bodhisattvas, śrāvakas, towns, hamlets, men and women of all ages, the Immutable Tathāgata, his bo-tree and beautiful lotus blossoms, which were used to perform the Buddha work of salvation in the ten directions, as well as the three flights of gemmed steps linking Jambudvīpa (our earth) with

[1] i.e. the cakravāla which forms the periphery of the world of Profound Joy.

Trayastriṁśās[1] by which the devas descended to earth to pay reverence to the Immutable Tathāgata and to listen to his Dharma, and by which men ascended to Trayastriṁśās to see the devas. All this was the product of countless merits of the realm of Profound Joy, from the Akaniṣṭha heaven[2] above to the seas below[3] and was lifted by Vimalakīrti with his right hand with the same ease with which a potter raises his wheel, taking everything to earth to show it to the assembly as if showing his own head-dress.

Vimalakīrti then entered the state of samādhi and used his supramundane power to take with his right hand the world of Profound Joy which he placed on earth. The Bodhisattvas, śrāvakas and some devas who had realized supramundane powers said to to their Buddha: "World Honoured One, who is taking us away? Will you please protect us?" The Immutable Buddha said: "This is not done by me but by Vimalakīrti who is using his supramundane power." But those who had not won supramundane powers neither knew nor felt that they had changed place. The world of Profound Joy neither expanded nor shrank after landing on the earth which was neither compressed nor straitened, remaining unchanged as before.

Thereat, Śākyamuni Buddha said to the assembly: "Look at the Immutable Tathāgata of the land of Profound Joy which is majestic, where the Bodhisattvas live purely and the (Buddha's) disciples are spotless."

The assembly replied: "Yes, we have seen."

The Buddha said: "If a Bodhisattva wishes to live in such

[1] Trayastriṁśās: the heavens of the thirty-three devas, the second of the heavens of desire.

[2] Akaniṣṭha heaven: the highest of the heavens of form.

[3] Sumeru has at its top Indra's heavens; below them are the four devalokas; around are eight circles of mountains and between them the eight seas, the whole forming nine mountains and eight seas.

a pure and clean Buddha land, he should practise the path trodden by the Immutable Tathāgata."

When the pure land of Profound Joy appeared fourteen nayutas[1] of people in this sahā world developed the mind set on supreme enlightenment, and vowed to be reborn in the realm of Profound Joy. Śākyamuni Buddha then prophesied their coming rebirth there.

After the (visiting Bodhisattvas had done their) work of salvation for the benefit of living beings in this world, the pure land of Profound Joy returned to its original place, and this was seen by the whole assembly.

The Buddha then said to Śāriputra: "Have you seen the world of Profound Joy and its Immutable Tathāgata?"

Śāriputra replied: "Yes, World Honoured One, I have. May all living beings win a pure land similar to that of the Immutable Buddha and achieve supramundane powers like those of Vimalakīrti! World Honoured One, we shall soon realize a great benefit resulting from our meeting and paying obeisance to this man now. And living beings, hearing this sūtra now or after the Buddha's nirvāṇa, will also realize a great benefit; how much more so, if after hearing it, they believe, understand, receive and uphold it or read, recite, explain and preach it, and practise its Dharma accordingly? He who receives this sūtra with both hands, will in reality secure the treasure of the Dharma-gem; if, in addition, he reads, recites and understands its meaning and practises it accordingly, he will be blessed and protected by all Buddhas. Those making offerings to this man (Vimalakīrti), will through him automatically make offerings to all Buddhas. He who copies this sūtra to put it into practice, will be visited by the Tathāgata who will come to his house. He

[1] Nayuta: a numeral, 100,000 or one million, or ten million.

who rejoices at hearing this sūtra, is destined to win all knowledge (sarvajña). And he who can believe and understand this sūtra, or even (any of) its four-line gāthās and preaches it to others, will receive the (Buddha's) prophecy of his future realization of supreme enlightenment."

CHAPTER THIRTEEN

The Offering of Dharma

THEREUPON, Śakra[1] who was in the assembly, said to the Buddha: "World Honoured One, although I have listened to hundreds and thousands of sūtras expounded by you and Mañjuśrī, I did not hear of this inconceivable sūtra of supramundane sovereign power and absolute reality. As I understand from your present preaching, if living beings listening to the Dharma of this sūtra, believe, understand, receive, uphold, read and recite it, they will surely realize this Dharma. How much more so if someone practises it as expounded; he will shut all doors to evil destinies and will open up all doors to blessedness, will win the Buddha's perfection, will overcome heresy, destroy the demons, cultivate bodhi, set up a place of enlightenment (bodhimaṇḍala) and follow in the Tathāgata's footsteps. World Honoured One, if there are people who receive, uphold, read, recite and practise this sūtra, I and my followers will provide them with all the necessaries of life. If this sūtra is kept in a town or a hamlet, in a grove or a desert, I and my followers will come to the place of the preacher to listen to its Dharma. I shall cause the unbelievers to develop faith in this sermon. As to the believers of it I shall protect them."

The Buddha said: "Excellent, Śakra, excellent; it is gratifying to hear what you have just said. This sūtra gives a detailed exposition of the inconceivable supreme

[1] Śakra: lord of the thirty-three heavens.

enlightenment realized by past, future and present Buddhas.[1]

"Therefore, Śakra, if a virtuous man or woman receives, keeps, reads, recites and reveres this sūtra, such an attitude is equal to making offerings to past, future and present Buddhas.[1] Śakra, if the great chiliocosm were full of countless Tathāgatas as many as the sugar canes, bamboos, reeds, rice grains and hemp seeds in its fields; and if a virtuous man or woman who has passed either a whole aeon or a decreasing kalpa[2] to revere, honour, praise, serve and make offerings to these Buddhas, and then after their nirvāṇa (death) should build with relics from their bodies a seven-gemmed stūpa as large as the four deva-heavens (put together) and of a height reaching the Brahmā heaven with a majestic spire, to which he or she will make offerings of flowers, incense, strings of precious stones, banners and melodious music, during either a whole kalpa or in a decreasing one, Śakra, what do you think of his or her merits? Are they many?"

Śakra replied: "Very many, World Honoured One, and it is impossible to count his or her merits for hundreds and thousands of aeons."

The Buddha said: "Śakra, you should know that if another virtuous man or woman, after hearing this sūtra of inconceivable liberation, believes, understands, receives, keeps, reads, recites and practises this sūtra, his or her merits will surpass those of the former man or woman. Why? Because the bodhi (enlightenment) of all Buddhas

[1] See also p. 36, n. 1 and p. 122, n. 4 about the sequence of the three periods of time (the past, the future and the present) which seems strange to modern scholars who do not know the profound meaning of Mahāyāna sūtras.

[2] The decreasing kalpa in which the period of life is gradually reduced in contrast with the kalpa of increment in which the period of life is similarly increased. (See the Abhidharma-kośa-śāstra.)

originates from this Dharma, and since enlightenment is beyond all measuring, the merits of this sūtra cannot be estimated."

The Buddha continued: "Long before an uncountable number of aeons in the past there was a Buddha called Bhaiṣajya-rāja (whose titles are:) Tathāgata,[1] Arhat,[2] Samyaksambuddha,[3] Vidyā-Caraṅa-Saṁpanna,[4] Sugata,[5] Lokavid,[6] Anuttara,[7] Puruṣa-Damya-Sārathi,[8] Śāstā Devamanuṣyāṇām,[9] and Buddha-lokanātha or Bhagavān.[10] His world was called Mahāvyūha[11] and the then aeon Alaṁkārakakalpa.[12] The Buddha Bhaiṣajya-rāja lived for twenty small kalpas.[13] The number of śrāvakas reached thirty-six nayutas[14] and that of Bodhisattvas twelve lacs.[15] There, Śakra, was a heavenly ruler (cakravartī)[16] called Precious Canopy who possessed all the seven treasures and was the guardian of four heavens.

[1] Tathāgata: the Absolute who comes as do all the Buddhas. See also p. 113, n. 2.

[2] Arhat: worthy of worship.

[3] Samyaksambuddha: omniscient.

[4] Vidyā-caraṅa-saṁpanna: knowledge-conduct-perfect.

[5] Sugata: well-departed.

[6] Lokavid: knower of the world.

[7] Anuttara: the unsurpassed one.

[8] Puruṣa-damya-sārathi: the tamer of passions.

[9] Śāstā devamanuṣyāṇām: teacher of devas and men.

[10] Buddha-lokanātha or Bhagavān: World Honoured One. The above nn. 1 to 10 are the ten titles of a full-fledged Buddha.

[11] Mahāvyūha: great glorious.

[12] Alaṁkārakakalpa: glorious kalpa.

[13] Small kalpa (antarakalpa): according to the Abhidharma-kośa-śāstra, a small kalpa is a period in which human life increases by one year a century till it reaches 84,000; then it is reduced at the same rate till the life-period reaches ten years; these two are each a small kalpa, but some reckon the two together as one small kalpa.

[14] Nayuta: see p. 126, n. 1.

[15] Lac: a hundred thousand or any large indefinite number.

[16] Cakravartī: a god the wheels of whose chariot roll everywhere without hindrance.

He had a thousand sons who were respectable and brave and had overcome all opposition.

"At the time Precious Canopy and his retinue had worshipped and made offerings to the Tathāgata Bhaiṣajyarāja for five aeons after which he said to his thousand sons: 'You should respectfully make offerings to the Buddha as I have done.' Obeying their father's order they made offerings to the Tathāgata Bhaiṣajya for five aeons after which one of the sons called Lunar Canopy, while alone, thought: 'Is there some other form of offering surpassing what we have made up to now?' Under the influence of the Buddha's transcendental power a deva in the sky said: 'Virtuous man, the offering of Dharma surpasses all other forms of offering.' Lunar Canopy asked: 'What is this offering of Dharma?' The deva replied: 'Go and ask the Tathāgata Bhaiṣajya who will explain it fully.'

"Thereupon, Lunar Canopy came to the Tathāgata Bhaiṣajya, bowed his head at his feet and stood at his side, asking: 'World Honoured One, (I have heard that) the offering of Dharma surpasses all other forms of offering; what is the offering of Dharma?'

"The Tathāgata replied: 'Virtuous one, the offering of Dharma is preached by all Buddhas in profound sūtras but it is hard for worldly men to believe and accept it as its meaning is subtle and not easily detected, for it is spotless in its purity and cleanness. It is beyond the reach of thinking and discriminating; it contains the treasury of the Bodhisattva's Dharma store and is sealed by the Dhāraṇī-symbol;[1] it never backslides for it achieves the six perfections (pāramitās), discerns the difference between various meanings, is in line with the bodhi Dharma, is at the top of all sūtras,

[1] Dhāraṇī symbol: stabilizer or power to lay hold of the good so that it cannot be lost and likewise of the evil so that it cannot arise.

helps people to enter upon great kindness and great compassion, to keep from demons and perverse views, and to conform with the law of causality and the teaching on the unreality of an ego, a man, a living being and life[1] and on voidness, formlessness, non-creating and non-uprising.[2] It enables living beings to sit in a bodhimaṇḍala[3] to turn the wheel of the law. It is praised and honoured by heavenly dragons, gandharvas, etc.[4] It can help living beings to reach the Buddha's Dharma store and gather all knowledge (sarvajña realized by) saints and sages, preach the path followed by all Bodhisattvas, rely on the reality underlying all things, proclaim the (doctrine of) impermanence, suffering, voidness and absence of ego and nirvāṇa. It can save all living beings who have broken the precepts and keep in awe all demons, heretics and greedy people. It is praised by the Buddhas, saints and sages for it wipes out suffering from birth and death, proclaims the joy in nirvāṇa as preached by past, future and present Buddhas in the ten directions.

"If a listener after hearing about this sūtra, believes, understands, receives, upholds, reads and recites it and uses appropriate methods (upāya) to preach it clearly to others, this upholding of the Dharma is called the offering of Dharma.

"Further, the practice of all Dharmas as preached, to keep in line with the doctrine of the twelve links in the chain of existence, to wipe out all heterodox views, to achieve the

[1] The illusion of an ego, a man, a living being and a life as taught in the Diamond Sūtra. See Ch'an and Zen Teaching, first series, p. 161, n. 6. (Rider, London; Shambala, Berkeley.)

[2] Voidness, formlessness and non-creating with non-uprising are the three gates to nirvāṇa. See also p. 22, n. 1.

[3] i.e. sitting in a Bodhimaṇḍala or circle of enlightenment to turn the wheel of the law or to spread the Dharma.

[4] Gandharvas: spirits on the fragrant mountains, so-called because they abstain from meat and wine and give out fragrant odours.

patient endurance of the uncreate (anutpatti-dharma-kṣānti) (as beyond creation), to settle once for all the unreality of the ego and the non-existence of living beings, and to forsake all dualities of ego and its objects without deviation from and contradiction to the law of causality and retribution for good and evil; by trusting to the meaning rather than the letter, to wisdom rather than consciousness, to sūtras revealing the whole truth rather than those of partial revelation; and to the Dharma instead of the man (i.e. the preacher);[1] to conform with the twelve links in the chain of existence (nidānas) that have neither whence to come nor whither to go, beginning from ignorance (avidyā) which is fundamentally non-existent, and conception (saṁskāra) which is also basically unreal, down to birth (jāti) which is fundamentally non-existent and old age and death (jarāmaraṇa) which are equally unreal. Thus contemplated, the twelve links in the chain of existence are inexhaustible, thereby putting an end to the (wrong) view of annihilation.[2] This is the unsurpassed offering of Dharma."

The Buddha then said to Śakra: "Lunar Canopy, after hearing the Dharma from the Buddha Bhaiṣajya (the Buddha of Medicine), realized (only) the patience of Meekness[3] and took off his precious robe to offer it to that Buddha, saying: 'World Honoured One, after your nirvāṇa, I shall make offerings of Dharma to uphold the right doctrine; will your

[1] The Buddha said to his disciples: "After my nirvāṇa, you should rely on four things which will be your teachers: on the Dharma rather than on the man, on the meaning rather than the letter, on wisdom rather than intellect, and on sūtras revealing the whole truth rather than on those revealing part of it."

[2] The twelve links in the chain of existence mentioned at the beginning of this paragraph show that they are not created, and are again mentioned here to show that since they are unreal, they cannot be annihilated for their underlying principle is inexhaustible.

[3] i.e. meekness to accord with the Dharma but no entry yet into reality.

awe-inspiring majesty help me to overcome the demons and to practise the Bodhisattva line of conduct?'

"The Buddha Bhaiṣajya knew of his deep thought and prophesied: 'Until the last moment you will guard the Dharma protecting citadel.'

"Śakra, at that time Lunar Canopy perceived the pure and clean Dharma, and after receiving the Buddha's prophecy, believed it and left his home to join the order. He practised the Dharma so diligently that he soon realized the five transcendental powers. In his Bodhisattva development he won the endless power of speech through his perfect control (dhāraṇī—of all external influences). After the nirvāṇa of the Buddha Bhaiṣajya, he used this power of speech to turn the wheel of the law, spreading the Dharma widely for ten small aeons. Lunar Canopy was indefatigable in his preaching of the Dharma and converted a million lacs of people who stood firm in their quest of supreme enlightenment, fourteen nayutas of people who set their minds on achieving the śrāvaka and pratyeka-buddha stages, and countless living beings who were reborn in the heavens.

"Śakra, who was that Royal Precious Canopy? He is now a Buddha called the Tathāgata Precious Flame and his one thousand sons are the thousand Buddhas of the (present) Bhadrakalpa (the virtuous aeon) whose first Buddha was Krakucchanda[1] and last Buddha was Rucika. Bhikṣu Lunar Canopy was myself. Śakra, you should know that the offering of Dharma is the highest form of offering. Therefore, Śakra, you should make the offering of Dharma as an offering to all Buddhas."

[1] Krakucchanda Buddha: see Ch'an and Zen Teaching, second series, p. 29. (Rider, London; Shambala, Berkeley.)

CHAPTER FOURTEEN

Injunction to Spread this Sūtra

THE Buddha then said to Maitreya: "Maitreya, I now entrust you with the Dharma of supreme enlightenment which I have collected during countless aeons. In the third (and last) period of the Buddha kalpa[1] you should use transcendental power to proclaim widely in Jambudvīpa (the earth) (profound) sūtras such as this one, without allowing them to be discontinued. For in future generations there will be virtuous men and women, as well as heavenly dragons, ghosts, spirits, gandharvas,[2] and rakṣasas[3] who will take pleasure in the great Dharma and will set their minds on the quest of supreme enlightenment; if they do not hear about such sūtras they will miss a great advantage. For these people are fond of and believe in these sūtras, which they will readily accept by placing them on their heads and which they will widely proclaim for the profit of living beings.

"Maitreya, you should know that there are two categories of Bodhisattvas: those who prefer proud words and a racy style, and those who are not afraid (of digging out) the profound meanings which they can penetrate. Fondness of proud words and a racy style denotes the superficiality of a

[1] After the Buddha's nirvāṇa the first period of the Buddha-kalpa is the first 500 years of correct doctrine, the second is the 1,000 years of semblance law or approximation to the doctrine, and the third is 10,000 years of decline and termination.

[2] Gandharvas: see p. 132, n. 4.

[3] Rakṣasas: malignant spirits.

newly initiated Bodhisattva; but he who, after hearing about the freedom from infection and bondage as taught in profound sūtras, is not afraid of their deep meanings which he strives to master, thereby developing a pure mind to receive, keep, read, recite and practise (the Dharma) as preached is a Bodhisattva who has trained for a long time.

"Maitreya, there are two classes of newly initiated Bodhisattvas who cannot understand very deep Dharmas: those who have not heard about profound sūtras and who, giving way to fear and suspicion, cannot keep them but indulge in slandering them, saying: 'I have never heard about them; where do they come from?', and those who refuse to call on, respect and make offerings to the preachers of profound sūtras or who find fault with the latter; these are two classes of newly initiated Bodhisattvas who cannot control their minds when hearing the deep Dharma, thereby harming themselves.

"Maitreya, further, there are two categories of Bodhisattvas who harm themselves and fail to realize the patient endurance of the uncreate in spite of their belief and understanding of the deep Dharma: they are (firstly) those who belittle newly initiated Bodhisattvas and do not teach and guide them; and (secondly) those who, despite their faith in the deep Dharma, still give rise to discrimination between form and formlessness."[1]

After hearing the Buddha expound the Dharma, Maitreya said: "World Honoured One, I have not heard all this before. As you have said, I shall keep from these evils and uphold the Dharma of supreme enlightenment which the Tathāgata

[1] Reality is beyond the duality of form and formlessness but this category of Bodhisattvas still gives rise to these two extremes which show their attachment to the subtle duality of ego and object. See Ch'an and Zen Teaching, first series, part III, *The Diamond Cutter of Doubt.* (Rider, London; Shambala, Berkeley.)

has collected during countless aeons. In future, if there are virtuous men and women who seek for Mahāyāna, I shall see to it that this sūtra will be placed in their hands, and shall use transcendental power to make them remember it so that they can receive, keep, read, recite and proclaim it widely.

"World Honoured One, in the coming Dharma ending age, if there are those who can receive, keep, read and recite this sūtra and expound it widely, they will do so under the influence of my transcendental power."

The Buddha said: "Excellent, Maitreya, excellent; as you have said, I will help you achieve this great joy."

At that, all the Bodhisattvas in the assembly brought their palms together and said to the Buddha: "After your nirvāṇa, we will also proclaim this Dharma of supreme enlightenment widely in the ten directions and will guide preachers of Dharma to obtain this sūtra."

The four kings of devas said to the Buddha: "World Honoured One, in all towns and villages, in the groves and wilderness, and where there is this sūtra and people reading, reciting, explaining and proclaiming it, I will lead local officials to go to their places to listen to the Dharma and to protect them so that no one dares to come within one hundred yojanas[1] of their places to trouble them."

The Buddha then said to Ānanda: "Ānanda, you too should receive, keep and spread this sūtra widely."

"Ānanda said: "Yes, World Honoured One, I have received this sūtra and will keep it. What is its title?"

The Buddha said: "Ānanda, its title is '*The Sūtra spoken by Vimalakīrti*', or '*The Inconceivable Door to Liberation*', under which you should receive and keep it."

[1] Yojana: see p. 64, n. 2.

After the Buddha had expounded this sūtra, the old upāsaka Vimalakīrti, Mañjuśrī, Śāriputra, Ānanda and others as well as devas, asuras and all those present were filled with joy; believed, received and kept it; paid reverence and went away.

Glossary

Akaniṣṭa heaven: the highest of the heavens of form.

Akṣobhya: the Immutable Buddha of the realm of Profound Joy in the Eastern region.

Alaṁkārakakalpa: the glorious aeon of the Buddha Bhaiṣajya-rāja.

Amalā: a fruit like the betel nut, used as a cure for colds.

Āmra park: (Āmravana), a wild-plum grove presented to the Buddha by a woman devotee called Āmradārikā.

Ānanda: young brother of Devadatta and cousin of the Buddha. He was noted as the most learned disciple of the Buddha, and famed for hearing and remembering His teaching. He was the compiler of sūtras and second patriarch of the Ch'an (zen) sect.

Aniruddha: one of the chief disciples of the Buddha; he was considered supreme in deva sight, or unlimited vision.

Anuttara: one of the ten titles of a full-fledged Buddha which means "the unsurpassed one".

Anuttara-samyak-saṁbodhi: perfect universal enlightenment; supreme enlightenment; omniscience.

Arhat: a saintly man, the highest type or ideal saint in Hīnayāna in contrast with a Bodhisattva as the saint in Mahāyāna; one of the ten titles of a full-fledged Buddha, which means "worthy of worship".

Aṣṭa-mārga: the eightfold noble path: correct views, correct thought, correct speech, correct conduct, correct livelihood, correct efforts, correct mindfulness and correct meditation.

Asura: a titan.

Āveṇikadharma: see "Characteristics of a Buddha, the eighteen unsurpassed".

Avīci hell: a hell which is ceaseless in five respects (karma and its effects are an endless chain with no escape; it is timeless; its life is uninterrupted; its sufferings are endless; and it is ceaselessly full) resulting from five deadly sins (parricide, matricide, killing an arhat, shedding the blood of a Buddha, and destroying the harmony of the Saṅgha).

Avidyā: ignorance, unenlightenment.

Bhagavat or Bhagavān: World Honoured One, one of the ten titles of a full-fledged Buddha.

Bhaiṣajya Buddha: his full name is Bhaiṣajya-guru-vaiḍūrya-prabhāsa, the Buddha of Medicine, who heals all diseases, including the disease of ignorance. He is associated with the East and his twelve vows are: 1, to shine upon all beings with his bright light; 2, to reveal his great power to save all beings; 3, to fulfil the wishes of all beings; 4, to cause all beings to enter the Great Vehicle; 5, to enable all beings to observe all the precepts; 6, to heal all those whose senses are imperfect; 7, to remove all diseases and give comfort to body and mind thus bringing all to supreme enlightenment; 8, to transform women into men (in the next transmigration); 9, to enable all beings to escape false doctrines and bonds in order to agree with the truth; 10, to enable all beings to escape from corrupt rulers and evil doers; 11, to give good food and drink to those who are hungry and thirsty: and 12, good garments to the naked.

Bhikṣu: a Buddhist monk.

Bhikṣuṇī: a Buddhist nun.

Bhūtatathatā: bhūta is substance, that which exists; tathatā is suchness, thusness, i.e. such is its nature. It means the real, thus always, or eternally so; i.e. reality as contrasted with unreality, or appearance, and the unchanging or immutable as contrasted with form and phenomena.

Bodhi: enlightenment.

Bodhimaṇḍala: a circle, holy site or place of enlightenment; the place where the Buddha or a master attains bodhi; a place for realizing the Buddha truth; a place for teaching or learning the

Dharma; a place where a Bodhisattva appears and where devotees have glimpses of him, for instance, Mount O Mei, in Western China, which is the bodhimaṇḍala of Samantabhadra Bodhisattva; Wu T'ai Shan, or the Five-peaked mountain in North China, that of Mañjuśrī; P'u T'o Island, off Ningpo, East China, that of Avalokiteśvara Bodhisattva; and Ts'ao Ch'i in Kuang Tung, South China, that of the Sixth Patriarch. A monastery where a monk awakens to the Dharma is a bodhimaṇḍala.

Bodhisattva: a Mahāyānist seeking enlightenment to enlighten others; he is devoid of egotism and devoted to helping all living beings.

Brahmā: the father of all living beings, a protector of the Buddha Dharma. In Indian religion, the Trimūrti or Trinity of Brahmā, Vishṇu and Śiva, is considered as an inseparable unity of three principles of creation, preservation and destruction.

Buddha: the enlightened one; one of the ten titles of a full-fledged Buddha; it is placed first in the triratna or Triple Gem.

Buddha kalpa: after the Buddha's nirvāṇa, the first period of the Buddha kalpa is the first 500 years of correct doctrine; the second is the 1,000 years of semblance law or approximation to the doctrine; and the third is 10,000 years of decline and termination.

Buddha-lokanātha: or Bhagavān, one of the ten titles of a full-fledged Buddha which means "Buddha, the World Honoured One".

Cakravartī: a world ruler the wheels of whose chariot roll everywhere without hindrance. The symbol is the cakra or disc, which is of four kinds indicating the rank, i.e. gold, silver, copper or iron, the iron cakravartī ruling over one continent, the south; the copper, over two, east and south; the silver, over three, east, west and south; the golden being supreme over all the four continents. The term is also applied to the gods over a universe, and to a Buddha as universal spiritual king, and as preacher of the supreme doctrine.

Campa: a yellow fragrant flower in India.

Canopy Lunar: a son of Precious Canopy who became Śākyamuni Buddha in the Bhadrakalpa or the Virtuous Aeon.

Canopy, Precious: an elder who was the father of 1,000 sons and became the Buddha of Precious Flame.

Chiliocosm, A Great (*tri-sahasra-mahā-sahasra-loka-dhātu*): Mount Sumeru and its seven surrounding continents, eight seas and ring of iron mountains form one small world; 1,000 of these form a small chiliocosm; 1,000 of these small chiliocosms form a medium chiliocosm; 1,000 of these form a great chiliocosm, which consists of 1,000,000,000 small worlds.

Dānapati: almsgiver.

Daśabala: see Powers, the ten fearless.

Dedication: see Pariṇāmanā.

Deva: a god, the highest incarnation of the six worlds of existence.

Devakanyā: a goddess.

Dhāranī (*or mantra*): an incantation, spell, oath; mystic formulae employed in Yoga, to win complete control over good and evil passions and influences.

Dharma: Law, truth, religion, thing, anything Buddhist. It connotes Buddhism as the perfect religion and is placed second in the Triratna or Triple Gem.

Dharma Eye: spiritual eye which is able to penetrate all things, to see the truth that releases men from reincarnation. There are five kinds of eye: human eye; deva eye or divine sight, unlimited vision; wisdom eye that sees all things as unreal; Dharma eye; the Buddha eye, the eye of the enlightened one who sees all and is omniscient.

Dharmakāya: the essential spiritual body of the Buddha, free from birth and death; it is formless and beyond the three realms of desire, form and formlessness; it is visible to Buddhas only.

Dharmaparyāya: the Buddha's Dharma-door to enlightenment.

Dharmatā: the underlying nature of all things; the absolute from which all things spring.

Direct insight: direct reasoning as contrasted with comparison and inference, comparison of the known and inference of the unknown.

Eight classes of beings who came to listen to the Buddha's preaching: devas (the gods); nāgas (dragons); yakṣas or demons in the earth, air and lower heavens; gandarvas, spirits on the fragrant mountains, so called because they do not drink wine or eat meat, but feed on incense and give off fragrant odours; asuras or titans; garuḍas, or mystical birds, the queen of the feathered race, enemy of the serpent race, and vehicle of Viṣṇu; kinnaras, the musicians of Kuvera (the gods of riches) with men's bodies and horses' heads; and mahoragas, demons shaped like the boa.

Eight Dharmas or devices to stop the morbid growth in this world in order to be reborn in the pure land: 1, benevolence towards all living beings with no expectation of reward; 2, endurance of sufferings for all living beings dedicating all merits to them; 3, impartiality towards them with all humility free from pride and arrogance; 4, reverence to all Bodhisattvas with the same devotion as to all Buddhas (i.e. without discrimination between Bodhisattvas and Buddhas); 5, absence of doubt and suspicion when hearing (the expounding of) sūtras which one has not heard before; 6, abstention from opposition to the śrāvaka Dharma (i.e. Hīnayāna); 7, abstention from discrimination in regard to donations and offerings received with no thought of self-profit in order to subdue the mind; and 8, self-examination without contending with others, in order to achieve singleness of mind bent on achieving all merits.

Eight forms of liberation (*aṣṭa-vimokṣa*): 1, liberation, when subjective desire arises, by examination of the object, or of all things and realization of their filthiness; 2, liberation, when no subjective desire arises, by still meditation as above; 3, liberation by concentration on the pure to the realization of a permanent state of freedom from all desires; 4, liberation in realizing the infinity of space, or the immaterial; 5, liberation in realizing infinite knowledge; 6, liberation in realizing nothingness; 7, liberation in the state of mind where there is neither thought nor absence of thought; and 8, liberation by means of a state of mind in which there is final extinction of both sensation (vedanā) and conception (sañjña). 1 and 2 are deliverance by meditating on impurity, and 3 on purity.

Eight heterodox ways of life: the opposite of the eightfold noble path: 1, wrong views; 2, wrong thoughts; 3, false and idle talk; 4, heterodox conduct; 5, heterodox livelihood or occupation; 6, false zeal; 7, wrong mindfulness; and 8, heterodox or wrong meditation.

Eight sad conditions: in which it is difficult to meet a Buddha or hear his Dharma; as hungry ghosts; as animals; in Uttarakuru, the northern world where all is pleasant and people have no chance to hear about the Dharma; in all long-life heavens, where life is long and easy and where people never think of the Dharma; as deaf, blind and dumb; as a worldly philosopher who despises the Dharma; and in the intermediate period between a Buddha and his successor.

Eighteen fields of sense: the six organs, their objects and their perceptions.

Eighteen unsurpassed characteristics of a Buddha (*āveṇikadharma*): as compared with Bodhisattvas—his perfection of body (deed), mouth (word) and mind (thought), impartiality to all, serenity, self-sacrifice, unceasing desire to save, unflagging zeal therein, unfailing thought thereto, wisdom in it, powers of deliverance, the principle of it, revealing perfect wisdom in deed, word and thought, perfect knowledge of past, future and present.

Expedient method (*upāya*): skilful expedient devices to expound the inexpressible and indescribable absolute Dharma.

Five aggregates (*pañcaskandhas*): form (rūpa), feeling (vedanā) ideation (sañjñā), reaction (saṁskāra) and consciousness vijñāna).

Five covers, screens or moral hindrances: desire, anger, drowsiness, agitation with regret, and doubt.

Five deadly sins: parricide, matricide, killing an arhat, shedding the blood of a Buddha and destroying the harmony of the saṅgha.

Five desires, arise from the objects of the five senses, things seen, heard, smelt, tasted and touched.

Five kinds of eyes: the human eye, the deva eye or unlimited vision, the wisdom eye that sees all things as unreal, the Dharma eye that penetrates all things, to see the truth that releases men from reincarnation, and the Buddha eye of the enlightened one who sees all and is omniscient.

Five periods of turbidity on earth (*kaṣāya*): 1, turbid kalpa, the origin of the first aggregate of form (rūpa) which continues for a period of time; 2, turbid or deteriorated views which correspond with the second aggregate vedanā or the responsiveness of the first five consciousnesses, and which rise and fall without interruption; 3, turbid passion which corresponds to the third aggregate sañjñā or the *sixth consciousness* that thinks wrongly; 4, turbid being which corresponds with the fourth aggregate saṁskāra or discrimination; and 5, turbid life which corresponds with the fifth aggregate vijñāna or consciousness which clings to form and mind as the basis of its existence. See also *The Sūrangama Sūtra*, p. 105, n. 1 for detailed explanation of the five conditions of turbidity. (Rider, London.)

Five spiritual faculties: see Pañcendriyāṇi.

Five spiritual powers: see pañca-balāni.

Four basic delusions: unenlightenment in regard to the ego; holding to the ego idea; self-esteem, egotism, pride; and self-seeking or desire, both the latter arising from belief in the ego.

Four Bodhisattva winning, or persuasive, actions (*catuḥ-saṁgraha-vastu*): 1, dāna, giving what others like, in order to lead them to love and receive the truth; 2, priyavacana, affectionate speech, with the same purpose; 3, arthakṛtya, conduct profitable to others, with the same purpose; and 4, samānārthatā, co-operation with and adaptation of oneself to others to lead them into the truth.

Four demons, of kleśa, of the five aggregates, of mortality and the heavenly demon.

Four infinite minds (*catvāri-apramāṇāni*), also called the four immeasurables, or boundless Buddha states of mind: boundless kindness (*maitrī*), bestowing of joy and happiness; boundless compassion (karuṇā) to save from suffering; boundless joy (muditā) on seeing others rescued from suffering; and limitless indifference (upekṣā) i.e. rising above these emotions, or giving up all things, such as distinction of friend and enemy, etc., thus wiping out all discrimination.

Four inverted views, of existence, pleasure, ego and clearness in saṁsāra in contrast with the transcendental reality of eternity, bliss, entity and purity in nirvāṇa as taught in the Mahāparinirvāṇa Sūtra.

Four kinds of Bodhisattva fearlessness: arising from his powers of memory; of moral diagnosis and application of the remedy; of ratiocination; and of solving doubts.

Four kinds of Buddha fearlessness, arising from his omniscience; perfection of character; overcoming opposition; and ending of suffering.

Four Noble Truths (*catvāriārya-satyāni*): suffering (duḥkha), its cause (samudāya), its ending (nirodha) and the way thereto (mārga). They were first preached by the Buddha to his five former ascetic companions and those who accepted them were in the śrāvaka stage.

Four states of meditation on the heavens of form: in the first heaven where the inhabitants are without the organs of taste or smell, not needing food, but possess the other organs; in the second heaven where the inhabitants have ceased to require the five physical organs, possessing only that of mind; in the third where the inhabitants still have the organ of mind and are receptive of great joy; and in the fourth they still have mind which is very subtle.

Four states of serenity (*dhyāna*) *in the formless heavens*: in the first heavens where the mind becomes void and vast like space; in the second where the powers of perception and understanding are unlimited; in the third where the discriminative powers of mind are subdued; and in the fourth where intuitive wisdom appears.

Gandharvas: spirits on the fragrant mountains, so-called because they do not drink wine or eat meat, but feed on incense and give off fragrant odours. See also the Eight classes of beings who came to listen to the Buddha's preaching.

Garuḍa: a mystical bird, the queen of the feathered race, enemy of the serpent race, and vehicle of Viṣṇu. See also the Eight classes of beings who came to listen to the Buddha's preaching.

Gāthā: poem or chant; one of the twelve divisions of the Mahāyāna canon.

Gṛhapati: an elder who is just, straightforward and honest.

Indra: one of the ancient gods of India, who fights the demons with his vajra, or thunderbolt; a protector of the Buddha Dharma.

Indra, The net of: hanging in his hall, out of which all things can be produced.

Jambudvīpa: our earth.

Karma: moral action causing future retribution, and either good or evil transmigration.

Karma of body and mind: the karma of body or evil karma of the five sense organs in the world of desire, and the karma of mind or good karma in the heavens of form.

Kinnaras: the musicians of Kuvera (the gods of riches) with men's bodies and horses' heads. See also the Eight classes of beings who came to listen to the Buddha's preaching.

Kleśa: trouble, anxiety, worry, distress, perplexity and whatever causes them.

Kumārajīva: an Indian Buddhist monk who went to China to translate Mahāyāna sūtras. Died in Ch'ang An about A.D. 412.

Lokapālas: the guardians of the world and of the Dharma.

Lokavid: one of the ten titles of a full-fledged Buddha, which means "Knower of the world".

Mahākāśyapa: a Brahmin of Magadha, disciple of the Buddha, to whom was handed down the Mind Dharma, outside of scriptures; the first patriarch of the Ch'an (Zen) sect; accredited with presiding over the first synod and with supervising the first compilation of the Buddha's sermons.

Mahākātyāyana, or Kātyāyana: one of the ten noted disciples of the Buddha.

Mahāsattva: a perfect Bodhisattva, greater than any other being except a Buddha, who is about to become a Buddha.

Mahāvyūha: the great glorious world of the Buddha Bhaiṣajya-rāja.

Mahāyāna: the Great Vehicle which indicates universalism, or salvation for all, for all are Buddhas and will attain enlightenment.

Mahoragas: demons shaped like the boa. See also the Eight classes of beings who came to listen to the Buddha's preaching.

Maitreya: the Buddhist Messiah, or next Buddha, now in the Tuṣita heaven, who is to come 5,000 years after the nirvāṇa of Śākyamuni Buddha.

Mañjuśrī: a Bodhisattva who is the symbol of wisdom and is placed on the Buddha's left with Samantabhadra on the right. His bodhimaṇḍala is on the five-peaked mountain in North China.

Māra: a demon.

Maudgalaputra: also called Mahā-maudgalyāyana, one of the ten chief disciples of the Buddha, specially noted for his transcendental powers.

Māyā: illusion

Merukalpa Buddha: a Buddha of a world in the east called Marudhvaja.

Mindfulness, Right (samyaksmṛti): retaining the true and keeping from the false.

Monistic form: a Mahāyāna term which means the one mind that creates all things.

Nāga: a dragon.

Nayuta: a numeral, 100,000 or one million, or ten million.

Nine causes of kleśa (troubles): misplaced love of real enemies, unjustified hate of real friends and irritation caused by one's own body are the three causes which, multiplied by the three periods of time, past, future and present, total nine causes of troubles, as explained by Kumārajīva who translated the Vimalakīrti Nirdeśa Sūtra into Chinese.

Nirvāṇa: complete extinction of individual existence, cessation of rebirth and entry into bliss.

Pañca-balāni: the five powers of faith, destroying doubt; devotion, destroying remissness; right thought, destroying falsity; concentration, destroying confused and wandering thoughts; and wisdom, destroying ignorance.

Pañcendriyāṇi: the five spiritual faculties: faith, devotion, right thought, concentration and wisdom.

Pañca-skandhas: see Five aggregates.

Pariṇāmanā: dedication here is somewhat similar to supererogation in the West but differs from it in that all merits derived from the practice of the Dharma are dedicated to the final realization of the Buddha's all-knowledge for the welfare of all living beings. Merits which are not so dedicated result only in self-enlightenment in the stages of śrāvakas and pratyeka-buddhas. Mahāyāna forsakes all merits in order to realize the absolute Bhūtatathatā which is free from dualities, relativities and contraries.

Patient endurance of the uncreate (anutpattika-dharma-kṣānti): rest in the imperturbable reality which is beyond birth and death and which requires a patient endurance without which thoughts will arise endlessly. The Prajñā-pāramitā-śāstra defines it as the unflinching faith and imperturbed abiding in the underlying reality of all things, which is beyond creation and destruction. It must be realized before attainment of Buddhahood.

Period of correct Dharma: the correct doctrine of the Buddha whose period was to last 500, some say 1,000 years, followed by the semblance period of 1,000 years, and then by the period of termination, lasting 10,000 years.

Pratyeka-buddha: one who lives apart from others and attains enlightenment alone, or for himself, in contrast with the altruism of the Bodhisattva principle.

Pūrṇamaitrāyaṇīputra: a disciple of the Buddha who realized arhatship by means of meditation on tongue perception.

Puruṣa-damya-sārathi: one of the ten titles of a full-fledged Buddha, which means "the tamer of passions".

Rāhula: the eldest son of Śākyamuni and Yaśodharā.

Rākṣasas: malignant spirits.

Ṛddhipāda: the four steps to ṛddhi or supernatural powers: intensive concentration; intensified efforts; intense holding on to the position reached; and intensified meditation on the underlying principle.

Right position, or nirvāṇa: should never be clung to for it implies a dualism of subjective ego and objective nirvāṇa which are precisely an obstruction to the attainment of the absolute state of suchness.

Sahā: our world of birth and death.

Śakra: lord of the thirty-three heavens.

Samādhi: internal state of imperturbability, exempt from all external sensation.

Śamatha-vipaśyanā: serenity and insight, or chih kuan; chih is quieting the active mind and getting rid of discrimination, and kuan is observing, examining, introspecting. When mind is at rest, it is called chih and when it is seeing clearly, it is kuan. The chief object is the concentration of mind by special methods for the purpose of clear insight into the truth and to be rid of illusion.

Saṁsāra: the realm of birth and death.

Samyakprahāṇa: the four right efforts, to put an end to existing evils, prevent evil arising, bring good into existence, and develop existing good.

Samyaksambuddha: one of the ten titles of a full-fledged Buddha, which means "omniscient".

Samyaksmṛti: see Mindfulness (Right).

Sapta-bodhyaṅga: the seven degrees of enlightenment; discerning the true and the false; zeal; delight; weightlessness; right mindfulness; serenity; and indifference to all states.

Śāriputra: a disciple of the Buddha, noted for his wisdom.

Sarvajña: all-knowledge, omniscience.

Śāstā-devamanuṣyāṇām: one of the ten titles of a full-fledged Buddha, which means "teacher of devas and men".

Seven abodes of consciousness: 1, the first dhyāna heaven of Brahmā when he was alone at the beginning of an aeon; 2, this first dhyāna heaven with his later creation there of his people, where bodies differ but thinking is the same; 3, the second dhyāna heaven where bodies are identical but thinking differs; 4, the third dhyāna heaven where bodies and thinking are the same—the above dhyāna heavens are the worlds of form; 5, 6, and 7, are the first three formless heavens as explained by Kumārajīva, who translated the Vimalakīrti Nirdeśa Sūtra into Chinese.

Seven categories of purity: purity in the precepts, in heart, in views, in doubt-discrimination, in judgement, in intellection and in nirvāṇa.

Seven riches: 1, reverent listening to the Dharma; 2, faith; 3, discipline; 4, meditation; 5, zeal and devotion; 6, abnegation; and 7, shame. The same term also means the seven ways of becoming rich in the Law, i.e. faith, zeal, moral restraint, shame, obedient hearing of the Law, abnegation and wisdom arising from meditation.

Shore, The other: the other shore of enlightenment as contrasted with this shore of suffering and mortality.

Siṁha: a lion.

Six heterodox teachers (*or six tīrthyas*) who were opponents of the Buddha: 1, Pūraṇakāśyapa who taught the non-existence of all things, that all was illusion, and that there was neither birth nor death, therefore, neither prince nor subject, parent nor child, nor their duties; 2, Maskari-gośālīputra who denied that one's present lot was due to deeds done in previous lives; 3, Sañjaya-vairāṭiputra who taught that there was no need to seek the truth because when the necessary aeons have passed mortality ends and happiness naturally follows; 4, Ajita-keśakambala whose cloak was his hair, and who was given to extravagant austerities; his doctrine was that happiness in the next life is correlative to the suffering of this life; 5, Kakuda-kātyāyana whose views changed according to circumstances; he replied "is" to those asking about existence and "is not" to those asking about non-existence; and 6, Nirgrantha-jñātiputra whose doctrines were determinist, everything being fated, so that no religious practices could change one's lot.

Six hindrances to the six pāramitās (perfections): stinginess, breaking the precepts, anger, remissness, confused thoughts and stupidity.

Six pāramitās or perfections: the six methods of perfection or of reaching the other shore of enlightenment: dāna-pāramitā or charity-perfection, śīla-pāramitā or discipline-perfection, kṣānti-pāramitā or endurance-perfection, vīrya-pāramitā or progress-perfection, dhyāna-pāramitā or meditation-perfection and prajñā-pāramitā or wisdom-perfection.

Six points of reverent harmony or unity in a monastery: bodily unity in form of worship; verbal unity in chanting; mental unity in faith; moral unity in observing the precepts; doctrinal unity in views and interpretation; and economic unity in community of goods, deeds, studies or charity.

Six realms or worlds of existence: 1, nāraka-gati, or that of the hells; 2, preta-gati, of hungry-ghosts; 3, tiryagyoni-gati, of animals; 4, manuṣya-gati, of human beings; 5, asura-gati, of titans; and 6, deva-gati, of the gods.

These are sometimes referred to as five realms, i.e. ways or destinies: 1, of the hells; 2, of hungry ghosts; 3, of animals; 4, of human beings; and 5, of the gods and titans.

Six supernatural powers (ṣaḍabhijñā): 1, divine sight; 2, divine hearing; 3, knowledge of the minds of all living beings; 4, knowledge of all forms of previous existences of self and others; 5, power to appear at will in any place and to have absolute freedom; and 6, insight into the ending of the stream of birth and death.

Six thoughts to dwell upon: Buddha, Dharma, Saṅgha, the commandments, almsgiving and heaven with its prospective happiness.

Sixty-two wrong views: which originate from the five aggregates considered under three periods of time. In the past each had permanence, impermanence, both or neither ($5 \times 4 = 20$). In the present, and here we deal with space or extension, each is finite, infinite, both or neither ($5 \times 4 = 20$). In the future each either continues or not, both or neither ($5 \times 4 = 20$), that is 60 in all. If the two ideas that body and mind are a unity or different are added, we have a total of 62.

Small kalpa (*antarakalpa*): according to the Abhidharmakośa-śāstra, a small kalpa is a period in which human life increases by one year a century till it reaches 84,000; then it is reduced at the same rate till the life-period reaches ten years; these two are each a small kalpa, but some reckon the two together as one small kalpa.

Smṛtyupasthāna: the fourfold stage of mindfulness that performs the fivefold Hīnayāna procedure for quieting the mind, and consists of contemplating: (*a*) the body as impure; (*b*) sensation as always resulting in suffering; (*c*) mind as impermanent; and (*d*) things as being dependent and without a nature of their own.

The fivefold Hīnayāna procedure to rid the mind of desire, hate, delusion, selfishness and confusion consists of meditation on impurity, compassion, causality, impartiality and counting the breaths.

Śrāvaka: a "hearer", disciple of the Buddha who understands the Four Noble Truths, rids himself of the unreality of the phenomenal and enters the incomplete nirvāṇa.

Subhūti: a senior disciple of the Buddha.

Sugata: one of the ten titles of a full-fledged Buddha, which means "well-departed".

Sumeru: the central mountain of every world; at the top are Indra's heavens, below them are the four devalokas, or the four heavens of the four deva-kings; around are eight circles of mountains and between them the eight seas, the whole forming nine mountains and eight seas.

Tao: a Chinese term which means road, way, path, doctrine, truth, reality, self-nature, the absolute.

Tathāgata: he who came as did all Buddhas; who took the absolute way of cause and effect, and attained to perfect wisdom; one of the highest titles of a Buddha.

Ten bonds: shamelessness, unblushingness, envy, meanness, regretfulness, torpidity, unstableness, gloominess, anger and secret sinning.

Ten evils: killing, stealing, carnality, lying, double tongue, coarse language, affected speech, covetousness, anger and wrong views.

Ten excellent deeds: 1, charity to succour the poor; 2, precept-keeping to help those who have broken the commandments; 3, patient-endurance to subdue their anger; 4, zeal and devotion to cure their remissness; 5, serenity to stop their confused thoughts; 6, wisdom to wipe out ignorance; 7, putting an end to the eight sad conditions for those suffering from them; 8, teaching Mahāyāna to those who cling to Hīnayāna; 9, cultivation of good roots for those in want of merits; and 10, the four Bodhisattva winning actions (devices) for the purpose of leading all living beings to their goals in Bodhisattva development.

Ten good deeds: non-committal of the ten evils: killing, stealing, carnality, lying, double tongue, coarse language, affected speech, desire, anger and perverse views.

Ten powers of a Buddha (*daśabala*) that give complete knowledge of: 1, what is right or wrong in every condition; 2, what is the karma of every being, past, future and present; 3, all stages of liberation through dhyāna and samādhi; 4, the good and evil roots of all beings; 5, the knowledge and understanding of every being; 6, the actual condition of every individual; 7, the direction and consequences of all laws; 8, all causes of mortality and of good and evil in their reality; 9, the former lives of all beings and the stages of nirvāṇa; and 10, the destruction of all illusion of every kind.

Thirty-seven contributory states to enlightenment (*saptatriṁśa-bodhi-pakṣika-dharma*): the four stages of mindfulness (smṛtyupasthāna); the four proper lines of exertion (samyakprahāṇa); the four steps towards supramundane powers (ṛddhipāda); the five spiritual faculties (pañca-indriyāṇi); the five transcendental powers (pañca-balāni); the seven degrees of enlightenment (sapta-bodhyaṅga); and the eightfold noble path (aṣṭa-mārga). See also detailed explanation of each separate group under its Sanskrit heading.

Thirty-two excellent physical marks of a Buddha: 1, level feet; 2, a thousand-spoke wheel-sign on feet; 3, long slender fingers; 4, pliant hands and feet; 5, toes and fingers finely webbed; 6, full-sized heels; 7, arched insteps; 8, thighs like those of a royal stag; 9, hands reaching below the knees; 10, well-retracted male organ; 11, height and width of body in proportion; 12, dark blue coloured hair; 13, body hair graceful and curly; 14, golden-hued body; 15, a ten-foot halo; 16, soft smooth skin; 17, the seven parts (two soles, two palms, two shoulders and crown) well rounded; 18, below the armpits well-filled; 19, lion-shaped body; 20, erect body; 21, full shoulders; 22, forty teeth; 23, teeth white, even and close; 24, the four canine teeth pure white; 25, lion-jawed; 26, saliva improving the taste of all food; 27, tongue long and broad; 28, voice deep and resonant; 29, eyes deep blue; 30, eye-lashes like those of a royal bull; 31, a white curl between the eyebrows emitting light; 32, a fleshy protuberance on the crown.

Three gates to Nirvāṇa: voidness, formlessness and inactivity.

Three indestructibles: infinite body, endless life and boundless spiritual possessions.

Three insights: into the mortal conditions of self and others in previous lives; future mortal conditions; and present mortal sufferings so as to overcome all passions and temptations.

Three poisons (or defilements): desire, anger and stupidity.

Three realms or worlds: of desire, form and beyond form.

Three states of sensation: painful, pleasurable and neither painful nor pleasurable feeling.

Three times: past, future and present which imply a duality of *is not* and *is*, the past which has gone and the future which has not yet come, standing for *is not*, and the present which does not stay, for *is*.

Three Treasures or Three Gems: the Buddha, the Dharma and the Saṅgha, i.e. the Enlightened One, the Law and the Order.

Three Vehicles (triyāna): of śrāvakas, pratyeka-buddhas and Bodhisattvas.

Threefold potency of a Buddha: the virtue or potency of the Buddha's Dharmakāya, or spiritual or essential body; of his prajñā or wisdom; and of his sovereign freedom.

Trayastriṁsās: the heavens of the thirty-three devas, the second of the heavens of desire.

Tripiṭaka: The Buddhist canon consisting of three divisions: sūtras (sermons), vinayā (rules of discipline) and śāstras (treatises).

Twelve entrances (āyatana): the six organs and six sense data that enter for or lead to discrimination.

Twelve links in the chain of existence (nidāna): from unenlightenment, disposition; from disposition, consciousness; from consciousness, name and form; from name and form, the six sense organs; from the six sense organs, contact; from contact, sensation; from sensation, desire; from desire, grasping; from grasping, becoming; from becoming, rebirth; and from rebirth, old age and death.

Upāli: one of the ten chief disciples of the Buddha, who was noted for maintaining the rules of discipline.

Upāsaka: a male lay disciple who engages to observe the first five rules of discipline.

Upāsikā: a female lay disciple who engages to observe the first five rules of discipline.

Upāya: expedient method of teaching the inconceivable and inexpressible Dharma.

Vaiśālī: an ancient kingdom near Basarh, or Bassahar, north of Patna, where people were among the earliest followers of the Buddha.

Vidyā-caraṅa-saṁpanna: one of the ten titles of a full-fledged Buddha, which means "knowledge-conduct-perfect".

Vimalakīrti: "undefiled or spotless reputation", a native of Vaiśālī, and a contemporary of the Buddha.

Wu wei: inactive, transcendental.

Yakṣas: demons in the earth, air and lower heavens. See the Eight classes of beings who came to listen to the Buddha's preaching.

Yojana: a distance covered by a royal day's march for the army in ancient India.